I0088825

TAKING CONTROL
OF
DESTRUCTIVE
EMOTIONS

DIEGO MESA

This book does not replace the advice of a medical or mental health professional. Consult your physician before making any changes to your diet or regular health plan.

TAKING CONTROL OF DESTRUCTIVE EMOTIONS
ISBN: 978-1-7360442-8-5
Copyright© 2021 by Diego Mesa
www.alfc.church

Printed in the United States of America. All rights reserved. This book or portions thereof may not be reproduced in any form without the prior written permission of the copyright owner. The only exception is brief quotations.

Unless otherwise noted, Scripture is taken from the New King James Version® (NKJV). Copyright © 1982 by Thomas Nelson. Used by permission. All rights reserved.

Scripture quotations marked KJV are taken from the King James Version of the Bible.

Scripture quotations marked NLT are taken from the Holy Bible, New Living Translation, copyright © 1996, 2004, 2007, 2013, 2015 by Tyndale House Foundation. Used by permission of Tyndale House Publishers, Inc., Carol Stream, Illinois 60188. All rights reserved.

Scripture quotations marked AMP/AMPC are taken from the Amplified® Bible. Copyright © 1954, 1958, 1962, 1964, 1965, 1987 by The Lockman Foundation, La Habra, CA. Used by Permission. All rights reserved.

Scripture quotations marked NIV are taken from the Holy Bible, New International Version®. NIV® Copyright© 1973, 1978, 1984, 2011 by Biblica, Inc. All rights reserved.

Scripture quotations marked ERV are taken from the Holy Bible, Easy-to-Read Version. Copyright© 2001 by the World Bible Translation Center. Used by permission. All rights reserved.

Scripture quotations marked (ESV) are from The ESV® Bible (The Holy Bible, English Standard Version®), copyright © 2001 by Crossway, a publishing ministry of Good News Publishers. Used by permission. All rights reserved.

Scripture quotations marked MSG are taken from THE MESSAGE, copyright © 1993, 2002, 2018 by Eugene H. Peterson. Used by permission of NavPress, represented by Tyndale House Publishers. All rights reserved.

Scripture quotations marked CEV are from the Contemporary English Version. Copyright © 1991, 1992, 1995 by American Bible Society. Used by Permission.

CONTENTS

INTRODUCTION

Everyone has good days and bad days; no one is exempt! On any given day, an individual can experience positive and negative situations, and how the person responds emotionally to the circumstances generally affects how he or she will view the day. Negative emotional reactions can be destructive and may impact a person's health, career, family, and loved ones.

Today, more than ever, people turn to medication, counselors, or various remedies because of the adverse effects of destructive emotions. The Bureau of Labor Statistics estimates that companies lose $3 billion a year to the effects of negative attitudes and behaviors at work. For this reason, the emotional well-being of people of all ages is being examined more closely today because far too many struggle with stress, anxiety, depression, strife, rejection, anger, negativity, fear, and so much more.

God created us with emotions; they are part of our makeup and God-given design. The best treatments to fight against destructive emotions are found in the Bible. Inspired by God Almighty, the words of His life-giving promises remind us that everything we need is available without limit to those who will come to Him for help. In Matthew 11:28-29 (ERV), Jesus said:

> Come to me all of you who are tired from the heavy burden you have been forced to carry. I will give you rest. Accept my teaching. Learn from me. I am gentle and humble in spirit. And you will be able to get some rest.

If you're tired and overburdened with life, Jesus invites you to come to Him and find rest. He will come alongside and guide you as you learn from Him.

It is my hope that you will take a leap of faith and discover, through the lens of God's Word, a clear picture of who Jesus is and His deep desire to see you totally set free from destructive emotions and find rest for your soul.

CHAPTER 1

SAY GOODBYE TO STRESS

Do not be anxious about anything, but in every situation, by prayer and petition, with thanksgiving, present your requests to God. And the peace of God, which transcends all understanding, will guard your hearts and your minds in Christ Jesus.

—Philippians 4:6-7 (NIV)

"I'm stressed out!" How many times a day do you hear those words? Perhaps you've overheard a friend, family member, work associate, or a passing stranger say those words today. You may have thought or spoken those three words yourself!

This silent thief identified as stress is just one of many destructive emotions waging war on our physical bodies, our minds, and affecting our emotions. Dr. Elena Villanueva, a holistic doctor, referenced a study published in JAMA Internal Medicine that estimates 60 to 80 percent of primary care doctor visits may be related to stress. In a particular study, only three percent of participating patients received stress management guidance.

I believe statements like "I'm so stressed out" or "I can't handle any more stress in my life" represent a cry for help. Although stress is intangible, it is a reality with a growing impact on our society. No age group or socio-economic group is off-limits.

What opens the door in a person's life to this invisible but larger-than-life force called stress? When stress enters, what happens? In this chapter, we'll answer these questions as well as present practical solutions.

THE CHALLENGE OF THE MARATHON

I enjoy the outdoors, and as a runner, I've participated in several marathons. As the signal is fired to begin, I'm filled with energy, my adrenalin is flowing, and I feel prepared for what's ahead. I set a particular pace when I'm on a flat road because I know how much energy I need to expend in order to keep going and stay focused.

When the route brings me to a big hill or a change in terrain, everything changes. I'm forced to adapt to the transitions along the way to keep going. My concentration, the level of energy I exert, my rhythm, my breathing, and my pain all intensify because that's what is needed to match the intensity of the challenge before me. Without the extra effort, I wouldn't be able to make it to the top of the hill or reach the finish line that waits beyond it.

By the time I cross the 20-mile point or realize that I've crossed the 22-mile mark, I begin to grow weary and feel as if I can't take another step. As I continue to move along, picking up one foot and putting down the other, I'm doing all I can to maintain a firm pace. Even though only a few miles remain, I can't reach the finish line without facing and conquering the challenge to complete the last few miles.

In many ways, everyday life has become the marathon braved by men, women, and children as each new day begins. When stress creeps in, it hangs around longer than many would like to admit. Before long, the anxious, busy lifestyle of the family becomes an uphill battle. Those who put forth the effort to overcome emerge victoriously and are rewarded, but the challenge can be difficult, and there are many who fold under the pressure.

THE PERFECT ANTIDOTE FOR STRESS

The Bible, our handbook for living, presents a message of hope to find real peace and rest from the storms of life, which often come in the form of destructive emotions. It's amazing how much the scriptures have to say about how to deal with feelings of being stressed out.

Jesus calls us to Himself, offering the promise of rest. In Matthew 11:28 (ERV), He says, "Come to me all of you who are tired from the heavy burden you have been forced to carry."

Jesus doesn't invite the perfect. He doesn't draw those who

have perfect marriages, perfect finances, perfect kids, or perfect health. He invites those who have struggles in their lives—those who are weary, perhaps due to health issues, financial struggles, problems with their kids or within their marriages. Jesus welcomes those who are heavy laden, which in today's world are those who are burned out and stressed to the max.

In verse 29, Jesus says, "Accept my teaching. Learn from me. I am gentle and humble in spirit. And you will be able to get some rest." In essence, we are urged to come under His direction and rule and to learn from Him. By doing so, we will find rest for our souls. He doesn't promise you or me that we'll never have to work or that things will always be easy. Instead, He told us we would find rest. He will revive you, strengthen you, and rejuvenate you. When things get tough, He will be with you in the situation, and He will make it easier to get through the difficult times.

As I mentioned, when I participated in marathons, the challenge wasn't at the starting line; it was about four miles from the finish line. When I crossed that 22-mile point, the real challenge began for me. I was tired, sweaty, and thirsty. My body was aching, and my feet felt like cement. But at that point in the race, something would happen. I would hear a word of encouragement shouted from the sidelines, telling me, "You can do it." Someone else would stretch out their hand holding a cup of cool water or an energy drink. After consuming the beverage, I would focus, with every ounce of energy within me, on the finish line four miles ahead. At that moment, I got a second wind, and suddenly I was rejuvenated enough to finish the race.

In the marathon of life, God is our source of rejuvenation. It's up to us to focus on Him, hear His voice, and accept what He offers. He told us to come to Him to find rest, and if there's anything that I recognize more than ever these days, it's that people need rest.

You and I, along with those around us every day, need rest for our minds from the pressures and stresses of life. It's not so much that our physical bodies get tired; our minds are overworked. We're bombarded by destructive feelings, which pave the way for stress. This leads to fear and frustration—emotions that steal, like a thief in the night, the rest we desperately need.

STRESS AND STRUGGLES

Stress is one of the weapons the enemy is using, and it is stealing the health of millions every year. Research has shown that heart problems, diabetes, certain infections, headaches, some forms of cancer, high blood pressure, insomnia, eating disorders, and digestive issues are often stress induced.

Stress can cause people to sweat profusely as well as twitch uncontrollably. You've probably noticed someone's eye or nose twitching constantly, typically a symptom of stress.

Have you ever encountered someone who seems to itch all the time or has broken out in hives? Unless the itch or the hives are caused by an allergic reaction, more than likely, it is stress related.

Stress can weaken the immune system, which enables us to fight against illnesses. Remember, 60 to 80 percent of doctor visits are stress related.

Health care providers, mental health organizations, professionals trained in psychology and psychiatry, books and other resources will tell you there are ways to manage stress, and, from a natural point of view, there are. Some offer techniques on coping with stress or finding temporary relief from its effects, but the results are based primarily on self-efforts and are seldom lasting. Unfortunately, stress eventually comes knocking again, sometimes resurfacing in another area of life, and the coping process and stress management principles are put in place again in hopes of experiencing some form of relief.

Today, people have more money than they've ever had before. They're more educated, have greater career success than they've ever known, and have more possessions than they ever dreamed of having. Many, however, cannot find one moment of rest for their souls. They're stressed out because of deadlines, demands, responsibilities, and expectations. They're stressed out because of losses, lack, and the load that they carry. They're stressed out because of the relentless noise they are subjected to day after day.

Without rest, without relief, stress begins to take its toll; wielding destructive blows to people's emotions and raiding their lives. Lou Holtz, a famous college coach, said, "It's not the load that breaks you down; it's the way you carry it." George Burns, a famous comedian of yesteryear, said, "If you ask what is the single most important key to longevity, I would have to say it is avoiding worry, stress, and tension. And if you didn't ask me, I'd still have to say it."

As followers of Christ, we do our best to stand guard against the so-called "big sins" like lying, stealing, adultery, and fornication, but it seems like we're less proactive in guarding against stress that potentially is doing more harm by stealing our health. Instead, we welcome it as if it's a normal part of life.

Stress is a subtle, devious thief in our world. We fail to recognize that it is probably a greater thief than any of the "big sins." We vigilantly stand watch at the main entrance as stress and a host of destructive emotions creep in the back door. We give our consent to worry and excuse the frustration and anxiety invading our lives.

When I consider this thief called stress, I'm reminded of Jesus' words in John 10:10, "The thief does not come except to steal, and to kill, and to destroy. I have come that they may have life, and that they may have it more abundantly."

THE ULTIMATE PRICE

The mind is the part of us that processes emotions, and it's a powerful part. When stress and fear are factors in our thought process, our imaginations can take us down a path toward destruction, painting awful images in our minds.

In 1991, scud missiles flew from Iraq to Israel. The death toll in one day rose 58 percent in that region. The increase wasn't necessarily because the scud missiles fell in a heavily populated area. The stress and fear caused by the bombs flying overhead triggered various reactions, including many heart attacks.

Kevin Carter was a Pulitzer Prize-winning photojournalist. He received the Pulitzer for a photograph he took in Sudan of a vulture stalking a starving Sudanese child. Kevin managed to scare off the vulture, but that image, as well as others, coupled with a lifestyle of "living close to the edge," took a toll on Kevin. A few months after receiving the award, at age 33, he committed suicide.

When Kevin's father was asked about his son's death, he said, "Kevin always carried around the horror of the work he did." It appears job stress, among other things, weighed so heavily on him that he ended his life. *(Retrieved from nytimes.com/1994/07/29/ world)*

The story of Christy Heinrich, a 95 pounds, 4'11" elite gymnast, is equally sad. Her lifelong goal was competing in the Olympics.

During an international competition in 1988, a judge said she was too heavy. After narrowly failing to make the 1988 Olympic Team, Christy, a much-disciplined competitor, placed fourth on the uneven parallel bars in the 1989 World Championships. Loved ones said she was never the same after the incident involving the judge. She became addicted to losing weight.

Dealing with ongoing eating disorders, Christy became weaker and frailer. In 1991, her worsening condition forced her to retire from the sport she loved so much. By mid-1993, she weighed 60 pounds. On July 26, 1994, at the age of 22, Christy Heinrich died of multiple organ failure, the result of years of eating disorders.

The words of that judge haunted Christy. A psychotherapist who counseled her said, "She was afraid of failure. She was terrified of being fat." The stress of it all resulted in her demise, robbing her of hopes, dreams, and a brilliant career as a gymnast. *(Retrieved from latimes.com/archives; nytimes.com/1994/07/28/obituaries)*

There are no easy answers for stories like Christy's or Kevin's. Stress and anxiety affects millions of people. Although they may share many of the same emotional and physical symptoms such as tension, headaches, high blood pressure, racing heart, rapid breathing, and loss of sleep, they have very different origins and degrees in severity. A person experiencing stress or anxiety must find an effective treatment plan to restore the body to a healthy state.

As a pastor, my heart is touched with a bit of sadness when I hear of people who have suffered loss because of a failure to understand how destructive emotions can drive someone to the brink of suicide. It's important to surround ourselves with strong believers who will support and pray for us and help us come through the dark tunnels successfully.

In John 15:5, we learn that a relationship with Christ is essential. Jesus said, "I am the vine, you are the branches. He who abides in Me, and I in him, bears much fruit; for without Me you can do nothing."

If your life is spiraling out of control, it's vitally important to refocus and gain the proper perspective. Don't allow stress and anxiety to derail your relationship with God. Recognize that you can't do life successfully without Jesus.

GOD'S ANSWER FOR SURVIVING STRESS

My son Adam gave me a stress ball for Christmas one year. It's an object that fits in the palm of the hand and is meant to be squeezed repeatedly. It's supposed to be a great way to help relieve stress, but I can tell you from personal experience that a stress ball doesn't solve all your problems.

Recently, I was squeezing the stress ball, and guess what happened. I squeezed it so hard that I broke it! All the stuff inside the ball fell out into my hand, and I had a hard time getting it off. Something that's supposed to help relieve stress created more stress for me.

Oftentimes, our approach to handling stress offers only temporary relief. For example, the overworked executive may say, "If I could just get away for a while and go on a vacation." An overwhelmed mom might say, "If I could have a whole day to myself and enjoy a massage and pedicure." You and I may say, "If I could just do this…or that…, everything would be better." Regardless of how you describe your perfect, stress-free environment, when the sun comes up the following day, you still have to face the issues of life.

When stress pivots to anxiety, then to fear, and you become

anxious about everything around you, it's time to stop and examine your life. The Bible is filled with promises to help you attain victory. Isaiah 41:10 says, "Fear not, for I am with you; Be not dismayed, for I am your God. I will strengthen you, Yes, I will help you, I will uphold you with My righteous right hand."

Fear is complicated because it can motivate us or paralyze us, depending on how we choose to approach it. As Christians, we must never allow it to dominate our lives. Christian author Corrie Ten Boom said it best, "Never be afraid to trust an unknown future to a known God."

Trusting God begins with taking the first step, which is to develop a relationship with Him. James 4:7 (NIV) says, "Submit yourselves, then, to God. Resist the devil, and he will flee from you." Isaiah 26:3 says, "You will keep in perfect peace those whose minds are steadfast, because they trust in you."

James 4:7 and Isaiah 26:3 give us the hope and peace of mind we need to be victorious over the chronic stresses in our lives. Meditating on them will help build trust in God, deepen and strengthen our relationship with Him, and conquer our fears. No counselor, psychologist, stress management program, or stress ball manufacturer can make such promises.

STRESSED BUT NOT FORGOTTEN

A great example of God fulfilling His promise to help when we're faced with a potentially devastating situation is the story of Job. Considering everything Job endured, I believe he had the opportunity to experience stress, anxiety, and depression beyond measure, and any other negative emotion you may want to include.

As we're introduced to Job, we see a prosperous man who was upright, feared God, and was blameless. Job was a blessed man, and probably the richest man of his day. According to Job 1:2-3:

> Seven sons and three daughters were born to him. Also, his possessions were seven thousand sheep, three thousand camels, five hundred yoke of oxen, five hundred female donkeys, and a very large household, so that this man was the greatest of all the people of the East.

As Job's story unfolds, this man, who was blessed with much wealth and success, comes under attack in various areas of his life. The Bible tells us in Job 1:14-19:

> And a messenger came to Job and said, 'The oxen were plowing and the donkeys feeding beside them, when the Sabeans raided them and took them away—indeed they have killed the servants with the edge of the sword; and I alone have escaped to tell you!'

> While he was still speaking, another also came and said, 'The fire of God fell from heaven and burned up the sheep and the servants, and consumed them; and I alone have escaped to tell you!'

> While he was still speaking, another also came and said, 'The Chaldeans formed three bands, raided the camels

and took them away, yes, and killed the servants with the edge of the sword; and I alone have escaped to tell you!'

While he was still speaking, another also came and said, 'Your sons and daughters were eating and drinking wine in their oldest brother's house, and suddenly a great wind came from across the wilderness and struck the four corners of the house, and it fell on the young people, and they are dead; and I alone have escaped to tell you!'

Considering that Job had only his wife left after learning about his tremendous loss, we'd certainly understand if he was stressed out, filled with anxiety, depressed, and greatly troubled. But instead of complaining and feeling sorry for himself, the Bible says in Job 1:20-21:

Then Job arose, tore his robe, and shaved his head; and he fell to the ground and worshiped. And he said: 'Naked I came from my mother's womb, And naked shall I return there. The Lord gave, and the Lord has taken away; Blessed be the name of the Lord.'

Now, if that isn't enough, shortly after the devastating losses, Job was stricken with painful boils from head to toe. His entire body was covered with sores, which were eating away at his flesh. As he sat on a pile of ashes scraping the rotting skin away, the Bible tells us in Job 2:9, "Then his wife said to him, 'Do you still hold fast to your integrity? Curse God and die!'"

Wow! That's not what the Bible says a spouse should be. A wife is supposed to be a *helpmate*, but what she said certainly wasn't *helping* Job's situation.

Job's reply likely wasn't what she expected. Job 2:10 tells us he responded by saying, "You speak as one of the foolish women speaks. Shall we indeed accept good from God, and shall we not accept adversity?" Furthermore, the verse states, "In all this Job did not sin with his lips." Job's response to a deeply disturbing situation is a remarkable example for us.

Three of Job's friends heard about his troubles, and they decided to visit him to comfort him (Job 2:11). The Bible reveals that as they approached, they were shocked by Job's appearance and didn't recognize him. When they realized it was Job, they wept aloud, tore their robes, and sprinkled dust on their heads (Job 2:12).

In the chapters that follow, we discover that instead of comforting Job, his friends said the sickness in his life was because of sin. They mocked him and called him a fool. Job responded by telling his friends they were miserable comforters (Job 16:2).

Taking into consideration all that Job suffered and what his friends determined was the cause of his condition, his response to them was nice. You and I may have said something else.

In his darkest, lowest hour, filled with stress and anxiety, Job didn't give up. Even after losing so much and the attack on his body, Job held on with steadfast faith; he continued to trust God.

Despite how Job's three friends treated him, the Bible says that Job prayed for his friends, and as he prayed for them, God began to heal him and restore everything he lost (Job 42:7-10). I love good story endings.

It's difficult for us to understand how a man like Job could go through that level of suffering and pain and survive with his sanity intact. Many have questioned why God allowed Job to be tested that way. However, the most important point of the story is that despite everything he suffered, we do know that the enemy did not have the last say in Job's life; God did.

We must continue to believe that it will never go the way the devil, our enemy, says it's going to go. We must trust that it will go the way God says it's going to go.

When the cares of this world are overwhelming you, consider what the Bible says in 1 Peter 5:7-10 (NIV):

> Cast all your anxiety on him because he cares for you. Be alert and of sober mind. Your enemy, the devil, prowls around like a roaring lion looking for someone to devour. Resist him, standing firm in the faith, because you know that the family of believers throughout the world is undergoing the same kind of sufferings. And the God of all grace, who called you to his eternal glory in Christ, after you have suffered a little while, will himself restore you and make you strong, firm and steadfast.

While we may never understand God's wisdom, we simply must trust His will.

According to the final chapter, Job reaped a lifetime of blessings after a season of distress. We're told in Job 42:12 (NIV) "The Lord blessed the latter part of Job's life more than the former part...." The attack against his life and the stress he endured was for such a short time in comparison to the 140 years he enjoyed after the affliction.

The Bible is filled with stories of people who experienced stressful situations. For instance, there's the story of Martha in Luke 10:41 which states, "And Jesus answered and said to her, "Martha, Martha, you are worried and troubled about many things." Verse 42 concludes with Jesus saying, "But one thing is needed, and Mary has chosen that good part, which will not be taken from her."

It's easy to lose focus, get distracted by matters that seem important, and miss the most vital part of the day, which is time spent with God. Choosing to be upset like Martha about having too many things to do is choosing to focus on unmet expectations and obligations, which opens the door to unnecessary stress.

Another instance involving Jesus is found in the book of Mark. We learn in chapter 4 that Jesus had been teaching all day. Afterward, He told the disciples, "Let us cross over to the other side" (verse 35). The disciples got into a boat, and as they went, they encountered a bad windstorm. The waves were breaking over the boat, which began to fill with water. The disciples were stressed and panicking.

Thinking the boat might capsize, they decided to wake Jesus, who was asleep in the back of the boat. The disciple said to Him (verse 38), "Teacher, do You not care that we are perishing?" In verse 39, we read, "Then He arose and rebuked the wind, and said to the sea, 'Peace, be still!' And the wind ceased and there was a great calm."

In both instances, Jesus took charge and calmed the toxic environment by speaking to the situation.

When we put into action life-changing scriptures by confessing them over and over, we can change the negative atmosphere called stress. The Bible tells us in Matthew 7:24 (ERV), "Whoever hears these teachings of mine and obeys them is like a wise man who built his house on a rock." And in Jeremiah 29:11 (NIV), it says, "For I know the plans I have for you, declares the LORD, plans to prosper you and not to harm you, plans to give you hope and a future." 3 John 1:2 (NIV) states, "Dear friend, I pray that you may enjoy good health and that all may go well with you, even as your soul is getting along well."

There are things we can control, and stress is one. Stress may come, but we don't have to allow it to stay.

DON'T DO LIFE ALONE

If anyone had reason to be stressed and filled with anxiety, it was the Apostle Paul. In spite of the numerous attempts on his life, oppositions, and persecutions, he wrote to Timothy:

I have fought the good fight, I have finished the race, I

have kept the faith. Finally, there is laid up for me the crown of righteousness, which the Lord, the righteous Judge, will give to me on that Day, and not to me only but also to all who have loved His appearing.

—2 Timothy 4:7-8

The Apostle Paul spent as long as six years in prison during his ministry. During the Apostle Paul's day, prisons were nothing like they are today, which include the basic necessities of life, like a toilet, running water, and three meals a day. Back then prisons were cold, smelly, rat-infested, and laden with disease.

There's no doubt that the Apostle Paul was subjected to a stressful prison experience. However, Paul didn't allow the stress of prison life to shackle and silence his thoughts. Instead, he learned how to remain calm and stay focused, trusting God during very emotional, unpredictable conditions.

I like to think that the Apostle Paul reflected on what the psalmist wrote in Psalm 62:1-2 (ERV): "I must calm down and turn to God; only He can rescue me. He is my Rock, the only one who can save me. He is my high place of safety, where no army can defeat me." In current terms, "Jesus is our stress reliever."

In 2 Timothy 4, Paul's message to Timothy implied urgency:

Be diligent to come to me quickly.... Only Luke is with me. Get Mark and bring him with you, for he is useful to me for ministry.... Bring the cloak that I left with Carpus at Troas when you come—and the books, especially the parchments. Alexander the coppersmith did me much harm. May the Lord repay him according to his works. You also must beware of him, for he has greatly resisted our words.

—2 Timothy 4:9-15

Within this passage of scripture are steps we can apply to overcome stress. The first principle is found in verse 9, which states, "Be diligent to come to me quickly." Paul was talking about Timothy.

If you and I are going to overcome stress, we must surround ourselves with the right people—healthy people. We need friends in our lives when we're feeling overwhelmed. I know that we may have many associates in our lives; I'm not talking about them. I know that we may have many acquaintances in our lives; I'm not talking about them either. I'm talking about the few people that we call friends who will come and visit us when we're held captive emotionally; people who aren't always trying to fix the situation but who will listen to us.

Paul, the man who saw miracles, preached the gospel, and authored two-thirds of the New Testament, was saying, "I need you, Timothy. Come quickly." If Paul needed a friend, then you and I do too.

There are times when we need prayer, encouragement, and the help of others. The lesson is simple: take note of Paul's words and surround yourself with the right people—healthy people. It's important to call upon those you trust; friends you can call at any time.

Paul knew he could rely on Timothy. He wrote in verse 9, "Be diligent to come to me quickly." Verse 21 (ERV) states, "Try as hard as you can to come to me before winter." Paul longed for Timothy's company and help, especially since several others in the ministry deserted him.

SAY GOODBYE TO DISAPPOINTMENT

In his letter, Paul mentioned Demas, a man who was once his traveling companion. Demas was a part of the inner circle— planning, praying, and working side by side with Paul. At one point, it appeared Paul and Demas would be a team for the long haul, but that was not the case. Paul wrote in 2 Timothy 4:10 (NIV), "Demas, because he loved this world, has deserted me...."

Paul acknowledged the offense he experienced when Demas deserted him, but he also understood the importance of not becoming stressed when disappointed. He was saying, "I'm not stressed out over Demas. I'm not even going to be bothered by Alexander the coppersmith who did me much harm."

Whether you like it or not, people are going to disappoint you. They are going to come into your life for a season, and then they'll be gone. When that happens, remember Paul's example. When he considered those who offended him, he said, "May it not be charged against them" (verse 16).

When those who are part of your inner circle disappoint you, don't get stressed out or become bitter. Guard your mind, guard your heart, and reflect on the good times you shared with those individuals. Don't get caught up in the disappointments because that can bring on stress and other destructive emotions. Cherish the relationships that don't frustrate you, and keep moving forward.

Know that sometimes we don't know the whole, untold story behind why people's actions result in disappointment, but it may be sensible to give people the benefit of the doubt. Consider that there may be valid reasons for their actions. This doesn't excuse what was done, but it may provide a broader perspective.

When my boys were young, they would occasionally get into arguments with their friends. When I would ask, for example, "Where's Johnny?" one would respond with, "I don't like Johnny anymore; he's not my friend. I'm never going to play with him again!" However, the next day, I would see Johnny and my child playing together.

Children have high tolerance levels. They don't seem to deal with relational stress the same way adults do. It's easy for them to forgive and move on.

Ephesians 4:31 (ESV) says, "Let all bitterness and wrath and anger and clamor and slander be put away from you, along with all malice." Philippians 4:7 (ERV) states, "God's peace will stand guard over all your thoughts and feelings. His peace can do this far better than our human minds." God's Word reveals the proper perspective we should possess when it comes to dealing with our emotions. It's up to us to act accordingly.

Through the years, I've experienced unpleasant situations in ministry and with associates; some were very hurtful and stressful. I never dreamed that individuals could behave in such an unkind manner.

After more than two decades in ministry at Abundant Living Family Church, there are people who have come and gone, and when I see them, I embrace them. Sometimes people have to remind me why someone left the ministry or what happened. I learned a long time ago that it's better to do life God's way instead of my way.

People of varying temperaments will come into your life, and some will disappoint you. That disappointment can evolve into anger, bitterness, unforgiveness, or have no ill effects. I encourage you to run your race well by trusting Christ who will give you the strength you need to act according to God's Word. As Philippians 4:13 tells us, "I can do all things through Christ who strengthens me."

When Luke wrote about a disagreement between ministers of the Gospel in Acts 15:36-41, he was writing about individuals who were once traveling companions. The account referenced the first missionary trip, which included Paul, Barnabas, and John Mark—Barnabas' cousin. During that trip, Mark deserted the team. There isn't much said about why Mark left, but it's certain that the Apostle Paul wasn't happy with his decision.

As Paul was preparing to leave for the other missionary journey referenced in the passage, we read that he asked Barnabas to join him. Barnabas was willing but also wanted Mark to accompany them. Paul and Barnabas had a "sharp disagreement" on the matter. The Bible reveals that strife came between them, and when they couldn't come to an agreement, they went their separate ways. Paul took Silas with him, and Barnabas took John Mark with him.

Amazingly, over time, John Mark matured, and Paul noticed the change. We see a great picture of reconciliation when Paul wrote in 2 Timothy 4:11, "Get Mark and bring him with you, for he is useful to me for ministry." Mark, at one point, was of no value to Paul, who wrote him off, but Paul was also able to let go of the past, forgive, and reconcile with Mark.

Don't become stressed when people don't measure up to your standards, ideals, or opinions. Like John Mark, you never know what's in them or what they may become. Don't get stressed out over people who don't always agree with you, especially those who seem to argue about everything. Paul had a strong disagreement with Barnabas concerning John Mark, but he got over it.

Guard your heart because if you get caught up in the unforgiveness trap, you may become judgmental and a very stubborn person. You may even begin to feel that it's your way or the highway, and that can be dangerous.

ACTIVATE YOUR STRESS RELIEVERS

In Paul's letter to Timothy, he requested that Timothy bring his coat to him in prison (2 Timothy 4:13). The scriptures basically reveal that Paul cared about his coat. Perhaps it was a gift, a favorite garment, or he may have wanted it to keep warm during the cold months. Perhaps the coat made him forget where he was for a moment.

When we find ourselves in overwhelming circumstances, it's important that we find relief from the stress by surrounding ourselves with things that comfort our hearts and bring peace and joy into our lives. We're all wired differently, and as such, there are different things that can help relieve stress and help us decompress.

For me, one option is listening to music when I'm driving my car. If I'm stressed about something, I play my favorite song repeatedly until I reach my destination.

Some reading this may think, *He's a pastor; shouldn't he pray if he's experiencing stress?* Of course I pray; prayer is my first go to for everything. I also believe there are practical things you and I can do to relieve stress. For instance, go for a walk, go swimming, or take up a hobby like painting, singing, or even dancing to relieve stress.

My administrative assistant, Connie, has a figurine on her desk of a church lady in a dancing pose as if she's praising Jesus. The inscription on the figurine reads: "Too blessed to be stressed." Now, that is the attitude we need to have each and every day. Psalm 150:4 says, "Praise him with timbrel and dance." Maybe right now is a good time for you to kick off your shoes and have a stress relief dance party.

JESUS, OUR EXAMPLE

In the gospels, we learn about the ministry of Jesus. He went about teaching, feeding multitudes, and performing many miracles for those who came to Him. Jesus opened blind eyes, healed the lame and the lepers, delivered people who were full of demonic spirits, and raised people from the dead. Wherever He went during His three and a half years, people surrounded Him by the thousands and came to Him to hear his teachings and receive an answer for their circumstances. Nobody ever handled stress as well as Jesus. He was always in control.

In the account involving Jesus in the wilderness in Luke 4, we learn that Satan tried to tempt Him three times. After each temptation, Jesus said, "It is written...." Jesus handled that stressful event by neutralizing it with the Word of God.

Speaking the Word of God is how you handle stress. You don't just have to sit there, take it, shut up and do nothing. We don't have to surrender to stress when we know what to do.

What comes out of your mouth during stressful times generally determines whether that feeling will weaken or grow stronger. Whatever situation, problem, or circumstance you are facing, let the words you speak reflect what you believe in faith, based upon God's promises. The Word of God, His promises to you and me, is unshakeable. His Word is more certain than tomorrow's sunrise.

Take charge of your life by memorizing and declaring God's Word. The following scriptures proved to be extremely helpful for mc.

"I will live and not die, and I will tell what the LORD has done."

—Psalm 118:17 (ERV)

"Little children, you are from God and have overcome them, for He who is in you is greater than he who is in the world."

—1 John 4:4 (ESV)

"But He was wounded for our transgressions, He was bruised for our iniquities; The chastisement for our peace was upon Him, And by His stripes we are healed."

—Isaiah 53:5

"I can do all things through Christ who strengthens me."

—Philippians 4:13

"For our light affliction, which is but for a moment, is working for us a far more exceeding and eternal weight of glory."

—2 Corinthians 4:17

"And we know that all things work together for good to those who love God, to those who are the called according to His purpose."

—Romans 8:28

PRACTICAL KEYS TO RELIEVING STRESS

In addition to the Word of God, there are practical steps we can take to relieve stress, including the following:

1. Eat Healthy

When you were fifteen, twenty, or thirty years old, it was nothing to eat hamburgers and fried foods. But when you approach 50 or maybe even forty, there may be consequences you never considered for eating that double cheeseburger or extra-large basket of fries. Overindulging may cause health challenges and require you to be on medication for the rest of your life. That's not God's best!

Do you want to relieve stress—the stress of not being able to move about like you used to, the stress of high blood pressure, or other stresses you're under? I recommend you consider eating right.

2. Exercise

There comes a time when you and I need to get off our blessed assurance and get our hearts going because exercise can relieve stress. And for the record, walking around the park while eating a donut and drinking your blended beverage as you talk on the phone is not exercise. Start walking, start biking, or join a gym. Whatever you do, get moving and start exercising.

3. Rest

Another great stress reliever is connected to getting a good night's sleep. Little children get moody when they miss their naps, and for adults, the benefits of getting enough rest are significant. Here are just a few reasons you should get enough sleep:

- Sleep has a direct correlation to heart health and preventing life-threatening illnesses.

- Sleep reduces stress and inflammation.

- Sleep enhances memory and energizes you to be more alert.

- Sleep helps your body repair itself.

4. Serve

Find a place to volunteer and serve others. Give back to your community or help someone who needs assistance. Giving to others meets a need in someone else's life, and it also helps reduce stress because we're focused on others rather than consumed with self.

BE ENCOURAGED

I'm a bit old school, and sometimes without realizing it, I find that instead of making life easier, I add stress to my life by doing things the old way. For example, before luggage had wheels, it had to be carried by a handle. There are still times when I travel that I pick up the luggage by the handle without thinking. If I'm traveling with my wife Cindy, she says, "Diego, there are rollers on the luggage. Why are you straining yourself so much? Just roll it." I'm sure most of us can identify with this example.

Instead of giving our stress to Jesus, regrettably, most of us carry the stress. We put off going to Him. We might not say the words, but our actions say, "Let me answer all my emails

first and return all the phone calls, and then I'll come to You."
"Let me post on social media first, and then I'll come to You."
"Let me eat breakfast and work out, and then I'll come to You."
"Let me complete my workday, and then I'll come to You." Then
there's the all too familiar: "Lord, You know my heart." The
bottom line is we go to Him when the time is right for us.

As I mentioned, Jesus had many opportunities to be stressed, such
as going from town to town, teaching all day, healing people, and
the other demands placed on Him. But Jesus knew the importance
of spending time with the Father. For example, in Matthew 14:23,
we read, "After He had sent the crowds away, He went up on the
mountain by Himself to pray; and when it was evening, He was
there alone." And in Luke 5:16, it says, "But Jesus Himself would
often slip away to the wilderness and pray." Mark 1:35 states,
"In the early morning, while it was still dark, Jesus got up, left
the house, and went away to a secluded place, and was praying
there." Jesus knew spending time in prayer and resting would
prepare Him to be effective in the work He was called to do.

As I stated earlier, we live in a stressful world that constantly
presents stressful situations. We are not promised a life free from
stress, trials, and tests. Like a revolving door, bad news is going
to come into our lives, but the key is not letting it stop us; we
must let it move out as quickly as it moved in.

God has promised, "I will never leave you nor forsake you"
(Hebrews 13:5), regardless of what life brings our way. Living
stress-free involves you choosing to invite Jesus to take charge
of your life. When you surrender your cares, He promises to

come alongside and guide you as you learn of Him.

We started this chapter with the foundational verse found in Matthew 11:28, which states, "Come to Me, all you who labor and are heavy laden, and I will give you rest." If you look it up in the original Greek, it says, "Come now!" It doesn't say tomorrow or next week. Even if you think you can handle the stress, don't delay, no matter how tough and strong you think you are.

Inevitably, the options we have when it comes to stress and its effects on us are surrender or survive; give up or persevere. The words of Jesus to His disciples remind us that Jesus had already won the battle for us when he said, "These things I have spoken to you, that in Me you may have peace. In the world you will have tribulation; but be of good cheer, I have overcome the world" (John 16:33). This verse offers a promise of rest, and I believe it includes peace of mind and emotional calm.

If you're stressed out, stop trying to deal with it on your own terms and in your own strength. Today, come to Jesus, give Him your stress and anything that concerns you, and He will give you rest. Life gets easier when we totally surrender everything to Him. Remember, you're too blessed to be stressed!

Prayer

Heavenly Father, I give You my stress today. I give You all my cares, all my worries, my marriage, my finances, and my job. I speak health and healing to any part of my body that is affected by stress. I cast my cares upon You, God, and I know that You are in control of my life, and I find comfort in that. Take all worry, unforgiveness, and stress out of my life now. I come to You, believing your Word that as I come, You will give me rest.

I thank You, Lord, and I trust You. I depend upon You. Lord, according to your Word, I will rest in You, starting today.

In Jesus' name. Amen.

Questions

What can you do to relieve stress in your life?

_____

_____

_____

_____

Have you had friendships that caused you stress? How do you deal with stressful relationships?

_____

_____

_____

_____

Jesus is our example of how to handle stress. What did He do that you too can easily apply in your life?

_____

_____

_____

_____

How can you encourage yourself and others when faced with stressful situations?

_____

_____

_____

_____

Additional Notes:

_____

_____

_____

_____

CHAPTER 2

GOD'S PRESCRIPTION
FOR DEPRESSION

I waited patiently for the Lord; He turned to me and heard my cry. He lifted me out of the slimy pit, out of the mud and mire; He set my feet on a rock and gave me a firm place to stand. He put a new song in my mouth, a hymn of praise to our God. Many will see and fear the Lord and put their trust in Him.

—Psalm 40:1-3 (NIV)

When was the last time you had a cold? Catching a cold is commonplace for most people, and unless the sneezing, coughing, and sore throat get worse, most adults just wait for the symptoms to pass rather than go to the doctor.

Depression in our current culture is similar to the common cold—likely to happen if the situation is right. But unlike the common cold, most of us will go about our busy lives unaware that we are suffering from the symptoms of depression.

According to Wikipedia, "Depression is a state of low mood and aversion to activity. It can affect a person's thoughts, behavior, motivation, feelings, and sense of well-being." People with a depressed mood may be notably sad, anxious, or empty; they may also feel hopeless, helpless, dejected, or worthless.

What's interesting to note is that adverse emotions alter perspectives, and oftentimes, those who think negatively believe that something bad will inevitably occur. Consequently, the fear of not being able to avoid or alter the probable event sets in.

The most commonly diagnosed form of depression is Major Depressive Disorder. According to the Facts & Statistics/Anxiety and Depression Association of America, around 16.1 million adults, age 18 years and older, in the U.S. have experienced at least one major depressive episode, which represents 6.7 percent of all American adults. The numbers are staggering and should give us pause to assess what we can do as a culture to change these statistics.

Unfortunately, the church hasn't always dealt with depression properly. Some have ridiculed people and told them they didn't have enough faith. Others thought they had demons or simply couldn't identify the issue.

For those suffering from this very real disease, talking with a doctor, pastor, or a trusted friend can be the first step toward recovery. The more we become aware and understand depression, the more likely we are to recognize the symptoms and take action against it. Depression is a real problem that has robbed many good people.

When we hear stories of well-known celebrities who ended their lives by suicide, it saddens us. They were amazing people who reached worldwide fame and fortune and brought laughter and entertainment to massive crowds. Unfortunately, they found themselves empty and lonely; individuals like Robin Williams, L'wren Scott, Don Cornelius, Anthony Bourdain, Kate Spade, Gina Allemand, and Lee Thompson Young, to name a few.

It may have seemed like they had perfect lives on the surface, but fame and success don't make you immune to pain and disappointment. On the outside, they appeared to be enjoying the things that success brings, but deep inside, they were desperate and overwhelmed.

Their feelings of hopelessness may have been related to a family trauma, financial trouble, health issues, loss of a loved one, career frustrations, or broken relationships. Whatever the challenges may have been, they turned destructive and led to an irreversible decision.

One of the most notable and encouraging stories I've ever heard on the topic of depression involves James Cash Penney Jr. At the height of his fame, this great philanthropist and successful businessman dealt with depression.

Threatened with losing his business, fortune, and family, J.C. Penney reached the end of his rope. He was admitted to Kellogg Sanitarium in Battle Creek, Michigan, where he received treatment for depression. Nothing brought relief to Mr. Penney.

One day Mr. Penney wandered into a cold, hollow hallway in the sanitarium where he heard singing. The sound came from the chapel where people were gathered singing a hymn he remembered from his childhood. The song's lyrics were, "Be not dismayed whatever betide, God will take care of you. All you need, He will provide, God will take care of you." As the words were sung over and over, it sunk into his spirit that no matter what he was feeling or facing, God was going to take care of him.

Sometime later, when Mr. Penney spoke about what happened that day in the sanitarium, he said, "In the next few moments, something happened to me...I believe it was a miracle. God had answered me when I cried out, 'Lord, I can do nothing. Will you take care of me?'" It wasn't long before J.C. Penney was freed from the depression he experienced. He went on to say, "I came out of that room a different man, renewed." *(Retrieved from JC Penney Story|Testimonies|fgbt)*

Many who struggle with depression turn to prescribed medications or the world's accepted treatments like hypnosis, psychoanalysis, and a number of new therapies available to treat this illness. More often than not, it's a hit-and-miss approach to see what works best. Sometimes people resort to self-harm by inflicting pain through cutting, burning, or bruising. There are also those like J.C. Penney who turn to God in times of desperation.

When you feel as if everything is falling apart in your life, remember that God is never far from you. Psalm 18:6 says, "In my distress I called upon the Lord, and cried out to my God;

He heard my voice from His temple, and my cry came before Him, even to His ears."

Know that it is possible to experience God's peace during the most difficult times in our lives. He desires to help and heal those who call out to Him.

A MERRY HEART

The Bible reveals solutions to fight against depression; solutions that go to the heart of the matter. Proverbs 17:22 (ERV) says, "Happiness is good medicine, but sorrow is a disease." This verse is essentially saying that a joyful, lively heart is beneficial to the body. It improves the attitude and brings a smile to one's face. The benefits are similar to what medicine is to an ailing patient. Adversely, sorrow of the heart breaks the spirit and sucks the life out of an individual.

Laughter and joy are effective solutions mentioned several times in the Bible. When I consider how God designed us, I'm amazed by the health benefits of laughter and happiness. Studies show that laughter releases endorphins in the body, increases blood flow, boosts energy, and diminishes pain. Laughter also strengthens the immune system, and can relieve stress for up to 45 minutes after a good laugh. These simple solutions are potent remedies that cost us nothing but to act. What's more incredible is that we can release laughter at any time.

Have you ever started laughing because you saw or heard someone else laugh? Most would answer yes because laughter, like a yawn, is often contagious. Laughter helps you relax, recharge, and it can change your perspective, enabling you to see situations realistically and as less threatening.

Today, more and more clinics are talking about the benefits of "laughter therapy," but this is not a new concept. In Job 8:21 (NIV), we read, "He will fill your mouth with laughter and your lips with shouts of joy."

I heard about a professor who asked psych students to participate in an exercise. He would call out words, and they were to say the opposite of what he said. The exercise began, and he called out the word "sadness," to which some replied "joy." He said "depression," and some said "elation." When he said "woes," there were no immediate responses. Eventually, one of the students yelled out, "Giddy-up!"

Today, it seems like many people have lost their "giddy-up." They've lost their "get up and go" in life. They don't have a reason to smile. They don't have a reason to be joyous. They don't have a reason to be hopeful. I believe we can all agree that it's better to be happy than sad. Proverbs 15:13 (NIV) says, "A happy heart makes the face cheerful, but heartache crushes the spirit."

When was the last time you belted out a robust laugh about something? How long has it been since your face displayed a genuine, ear-to-ear smile? There are those who cry when they laugh, some snort loud enough to make you look in their direction, and some slap their leg over and over when they laugh. Whatever your laughter style is, take time to laugh and laugh some more.

ROAD MAP TO DEPRESSION

In 1 Kings 18:21 (NIV), a bold prophet of God by the name of Elijah stood at Mount Carmel against 450 prophets of Baal who claimed that Baal was God. Elijah said to the people, "How long will you waver between two opinions? If the Lord is God, follow him; but if Baal is God, follow him."

The Bible tells us that Elijah told the prophets of Baal to choose two bulls, one for themselves and one for him. He instructed them to cut them into pieces, put the meat of one on the wood, but not to start a fire, and he would do the same. According to verse 24, Elijah said to the prophets of Baal, "You call on the name of your god, and I will call on the name of the Lord. The god who answers by fire—he is God."

For several hours the prophets of Baal tried to get Baal's attention, but eventually they gave up and Elijah took over. The Bible tells us that Elijah repaired the stone altar of the Lord that had been thrown down, dug a small ditch around the altar, and asked the servants to fill the ditch with water. Elijah put the wood on the altar and laid the bull pieces on the wood. In 1 Kings 18:36-40 (ERV), we read the following:

> At about the time for the afternoon sacrifice, the prophet Elijah approached the altar and prayed, 'Lord, the God of Abraham, Isaac, and Jacob, I ask you now to prove that you are the God of Israel and that I am your servant. Show these people that it was you who commanded me to do all these things. Lord, answer my prayer. Show these people that you, Lord, are God and that you are the one who is bringing them back to you.'

Then fire came down from the Lord and burned the sacrifice, the wood, the stones, and the ground around the altar. Then it dried up all the water in the ditch....

Then Elijah said, 'Get the prophets of Baal! Don't let any of them escape!' So the people captured all the prophets. Then Elijah led them down to Kishon Creek and killed them all.

Wow, what a miracle! I'm sure that amazing demonstration of God's power released through Elijah's hands fueled his emotions with exhilaration and jubilation. It was a moment etched in his mind he would never forget as he witnessed God Almighty releasing fire from heaven, consuming the sacrifice, the wood, the stones, and licking up the water from the trench, proving that He is the true and living God.

The story continues in 1 Kings 19:2 (NIV). Furious about what happened to the prophets of Baal on Mount Carmel, Jezebel, wife of King Ahab, sent a messenger to Elijah to tell him on her behalf, "May the gods deal with me, be it ever so severely, if by this time tomorrow I do not make your life like that of one of them." Basically, she was telling him, "What you've done to the 450 prophets, I will do to you!"

I wish I could say Elijah rose up and said, *Oh no you don't, Jezebel! Who do you think you are? The God I serve is all-powerful, and I have nothing to fear!* But instead, when the messenger delivered Jezebel's decree, Elijah was overtaken by fear.

The power that words have over us is incredible. Words we hear cause images to form in our minds, and these images can drive us to desperation which is what happened to Elijah. Instead of Elijah reacting like a lion who roars, he reacted like a turtle that tucks in its head and tail in fear. I'm glad the Bible reveals that even great men that God used experienced challenges just as we do.

Elijah was so frantic and frightened that he got up and ran for his life, leaving his servant behind. Jezebel's words kept echoing in his mind. He ran as fast as he could to Beersheba, Judah, which wasn't just around the block. He ran 80 to 100 miles away to escape Jezebel's threat. Based on how far Elijah ran, I would guess he was the first ultramarathoner recorded in the Bible (1 Kings 19:3).

Exhausted from repairing the altar, digging the trench, slaughtering 450 prophets, running 80-100 miles; weak from the sun's heat, and hungry, he found himself alone in the desert under a broom bush, and prayed that he might die. Elijah said (verse 4), "I have had enough, Lord. Take my life; I am no better than my ancestors."

Isn't it amazing that one moment you can be on top of the mountain of victory and success and the next moment plummet in a downward spiral?

Elijah may have felt as if he was going to die, but he didn't. He may have felt like quitting, but that wasn't a reason to quit. In his mind, he saw himself as a weak man, a failure, unworthy and hopeless. He was physically and emotionally drained, and instead of asking God to help him, he fell into a depressed mood.

Alone and dejected, Elijah fell asleep under the bush. The Bible tells us (verse 5) that while he slept, an angel touched him. The angel told him, "Get up and eat." Verse 6 reads, "He looked around, and there by his head was some bread baked over hot coals, and a jar of water. He ate and drank and then went back to sleep." He was so tired and depressed that all he wanted to do was sleep.

Most of us have experienced moments of low moods due to stress or lack of sleep. The body may react negatively during these periods.

God didn't want Elijah to stay there. The angel of the Lord came back a second time, touched him, and said, "Get up and eat! If you don't, you will not be strong enough to make the long trip" (verse 7). The passage goes on to say (verses 8-9), "So he got up and ate and drank. Strengthened by that food, he traveled forty days and forty nights until he reached Horeb, the mountain of God. There he went into a cave and spent the night." Maybe for a moment, he felt better, but he really wasn't better.

God knew that Horeb was not where Elijah was supposed to be. The Lord said to him, "What are you doing here, Elijah?" Elijah replied:

> I have been very zealous for the Lord God Almighty. The Israelites have rejected your covenant, torn down your altars, and put your prophets to death with the sword. I am the only one left, and now they are trying to kill me too.
> —1 Kings 19:10 (NIV)

The bold prophet who took on 450 false prophets decided to do a 180-degree turn and took on the attitude of a weak, "woe is me," pitiful man.

The outcome of every situation we encounter is dependent on

our response to the situation. In James 5:17, we read, "Elijah was a man with a nature like ours." He had the same strengths and weaknesses that we all have.

There are days we can be on the mountaintop and suddenly run in fear for our lives. What would you do if you faced a similar situation? Could you run an ultramarathon to escape that type of threat? You'd probably be surprised as to what you might do to protect yourself if something terrorized you.

People run away and hide emotionally from all sorts of things. Some people pick up and move from coast to coast because of a bad marriage, bad relationships, bad business deals, and a host of other challenges that bring on hysteria, fear, and depression.

The negative thoughts running through Elijah's mind got the best of him, producing his depressed state. He visualized Jezebel's threat as credible and ran for his life even though what he imagined never materialized.

I can remember a time when people wore mood rings; it was the 1970s to date myself. The ring would appear to reveal the mood the person was experiencing. The strange thing was that some individuals who wore the rings would act according to what the ring seemed to reveal. If the ring appeared to indicate that they were sad, they would act sad. If it seemed to suggest that they were happy, they would act happy. I often thought to myself, *Why don't people tell the ring what mood they should have rather than allow the ring to dictate their mood?* I believe it's better to be a thermostat that controls the temperature instead of a thermometer that merely displays the temperature.

COMMON CAUSES OF DEPRESSION

Fear

Did you know that fear can be attributed to depression? Being afraid of something, someone, or a perceived situation can negatively impact a person's sense of well-being. Keep in mind that there are favorable forms of fear, such as the fear that keeps us from engaging in dangerous activities or the fear we have for God, also known as reverence. However, phobias and fears that obstruct a healthy forward motion can drive some into depression.

Fear is a powerful agent, especially when it comes to decision-making. Fear has people not committing to one another. Fear has people not stepping into their calling or ministry. Fear has people not living out their days to the fullest because they believe what was said to them or spoken over them, or they believe a sickness will take them out.

My question to you: Has fear trapped you, paralyzed you, or disrupted your life? What scares the heebie-jeebies out of you?

Unfortunately, if people don't recognize where fear comes from, they will be defeated. The Bible tells us in 2 Timothy 1:7 (ERV), "The Spirit God gave us does not make us afraid. His Spirit is a source of power and love and self-control." So if God is not the source of our fears, where does it come from?

A. B. Simpson, a theologian, author, and founder of the Christian and Missionary Alliance, said, "Fear is born of Satan, and if we would only take time to think a moment, we would see that everything Satan says is founded upon a falsehood."

When we accept the fact that God did not give us a spirit of fear, we can look at fear and say, "You're just a spirit, and you don't scare me. God has not given me a spirit of fear, but of power, love and a sound mind. I bind and rebuke you, and I take authority over you now. I walk in the promise that God has given me of a sound mind. In Jesus' name!"

We are either going to fight against what intimidates us or run from it. You and I have to be individuals who fight. We must fight the good fight of faith and not allow fear to get the best of us. In Isaiah 41:10 (ERV), the Bible says, "Don't worry—I am with you. Don't be afraid—I am your God. I will make you strong and help you. I will support you with my right hand that brings victory."

When I was diagnosed with terminal cancer, fear got the best of me. But the more that I got into God's Word, the easier it became to break free from fear. When I fully realized what God's will was for my life concerning the sickness, fear began to leave. Eventually, I got to the point where I could honestly say, "Cancer, you don't scare me anymore. You will not take me out; you will not kill me."

Unfortunately, there are a lot of people who can't confidently speak to their situations because fear overpowers them. They haven't allowed the promises of God, the truths found in the Word, to override their fears. They haven't grown to the point where the Word of God is more real than the opposition they're facing.

When I was a little boy, I was deathly afraid of clowns. I didn't go to the circus because of those terrifying performers dressed as clowns. This specific fear is called coulrophobia which doesn't just affect children; people of all ages can suffer from this fear. As I matured into adulthood and became more familiar with God's Word, I overcame my childhood fears. But so many times, our childhood fears can grow to be adult nightmares.

Be encouraged! If you're fearful today, get into God's Word, find the promises that relate to the situation you're facing, speak God's Word over your circumstance, by faith, and watch the fear slowly subside and break off of you. God's Word is the answer to overcoming fear. The day is coming when you too can say, "I'm not afraid anymore, in Jesus' name."

Fatigue

Sometimes depression moves in on us because of exhaustion. We're tired, burned out, and feel like we're running on empty. More often than not, we don't stop to take a break or a vacation; we just keep going. You can see this in Elijah's situation. It took great emotional and physical energy to do what God told him to do. He was exhausted from repairing the altar, digging the trench, killing 450 prophets, and running 80-100 miles. Elijah was totally burned out, weak, hungry, and suffering from a lack of sleep. Can you identify?

In Psalm 42:3 (NIV), the psalmist wrote, "My tears have been my food day and night, while people say to me all day long, 'Where is your God?'" It's apparent that the psalmist was feeling pretty low. He may have been exhausted and completely overwhelmed.

Have you ever experienced a time in your life when you were so overwhelmed with sadness that food was the farthest thing from your mind? The things you truly enjoyed failed to bring a smile to your face. You lost your "giddy-up" and joy. Maybe the cares of the world became heavy burdens.

When we subject our bodies to overload, it stands to reason that we won't have the energy we need to go the distance. Suddenly, the small molehills in our lives become big mountains that are hard to overcome.

The thought of the psalmist continues in Psalm 42:5 (NIV): "Why, my soul, are you downcast? Why so disturbed within me? Put your hope in God, for I will yet praise him, my Savior and my God." The psalmist recognized that taking charge of his situation and choosing to hope in God would turn his sadness into praise once again.

Have you noticed that elderly people seem to take life in stride? Many have chosen not to worry about things that aren't important and have slowed their pace in life. I believe they have discovered that rest and extra time to complete tasks help restore the body's energy and mind. Most aren't rushed to do things in haste. Just drive behind an elderly person and notice the speed at which he maneuvers his vehicle. The person is in no hurry, and each move appears to be well thought out.

Instead of being the speedy hare, sometimes we need to be a turtle. Sometimes instead of being the thoroughbred racehorse, we need to be the country plowing horse. Instead of being the race car, be the pace car.

A laid-back approach to life may be just what we need, but instead, it seems like we're always running on fumes. We're like car owners who only take time to put in five bucks of gas when the tank is on empty. The reservoir is never full, yet we endeavor to see how far we can go time and time again. We say to ourselves, "Just a bit farther...I think I can make it past one more exit." But then we pass the exit and try to go even farther. Eventually, we become stranded on the side of the road holding the red gas can.

It's sad to say, but this scenario has become a way of life for many. According to a recent statistic on Americans, we work long days, take few vacations, and retire late in life.

In Genesis 2:2 (NIV), it says, "By the seventh day God had finished the work he had been doing; so on the seventh day he rested from all his work." If God took time to rest after His work, shouldn't we designate time to rest?

When we disregard God's law of rest, the body's emotional state will start to suffer. Lack of rest adversely affected Elijah's frame of mind, and fatigue opened the door to depression. God, after creation, didn't need to rest, but He was setting an example; a precedence for us to follow.

Isaiah 40:31 (NIV) states, "But those who hope in the Lord will renew their strength. They will soar on wings like eagles; they will run and not grow weary, they will walk and not be faint." When you follow God's plan of rest, your body will be refreshed physically, emotionally, and spiritually.

Frustration

Depression can also be linked to frustration which is an emotion individuals experience as a result of unmet expectations or the inability to correct an outcome. I'm sure we've all had to work through frustrations. Who hasn't been frustrated about unmet expectations?

There are those who'd say, "I should have been promoted by now." "I thought I'd be making more money by now." "I thought I'd be married by this time." "I thought I'd have kids by now." "I thought I'd be retired by now." "I thought things would be different by now." Those individuals are likely frustrated because their hopes and dreams haven't materialized.

Elijah's frustration and dismay were among the ingredients that fueled his depressed mood. He was focusing on the wrong thing. He probably said to himself, *I thought the country would have turned to God. I thought Ahab would have stood up to Jezebel. I should have stood up to Jezebel. I hoped that Jezebel would change her wicked ways.* His frustrations became a distraction that kept him from doing what God called him to do.

The Holy Spirit was laying out a plan for Elijah, but he wasn't following it. Instead of communicating with the Holy Spirit, he got caught up in his emotions. The LORD had to teach Elijah an important lesson—just because He wasn't working the way Elijah expected, that didn't mean He wasn't working. Just because things didn't change immediately, that didn't mean God wouldn't get rid of Baal worship and deal with Ahab and Jezebel. He would just use other people to accomplish His plan.

I'll be the first to admit that I have many weaknesses. One weakness of mine is impatience. When I was a young kid, I couldn't stay in my seat. I was a wiggle worm. I was impatient and always had issues focusing on projects, and that would really frustrate me. Without warning, I would turn around and hit someone, run, play, and tell jokes, all within a brief period. It seemed as if I lived in the principal's office. To be honest, I'm still working on being patient because when expectations are not met, or something is taking too long, I feel frustrated.

Not long ago, I received an emergency phone call. The situation described over the phone required me to leave my location immediately and drive to the hospital. I jumped into the shower, got dressed, got in my truck, and started driving.

The freeway was my quickest route, so I headed in the direction of the closest one. I turned onto the freeway onramp, and immediately noticed there was a log jam. When I looked a little closer, I saw about twelve cars waiting at the metered signal to enter the flow of traffic on the freeway, which was also backed up. I became impatient and decided to pull into the emergency lane. Then I began to think, *Do I want to continue and stay caught in this jam, or should I put my car in reverse and get back on the street where I'll bypass the traffic?*

I decided to put the car in reverse, but cars were approaching behind me by that time. I wanted to continue but had to wait for conditions to become safe enough for me to do so. Each time I tried to back up, another car came along, forcing me to wait. All the while, time was passing, but I was committed to my plan. My frustration and impatience had reached a level where I even considered making a U-turn on the onramp as another car approached, but I caught myself and said, "Diego, are you crazy?"

After little to no progress, I decided to just remain on the freeway. I continued, even though frustrated and impatient, until the metered signal allowed me to enter the flow of traffic. At that moment, I realized that I could have been a mile or more farther down the freeway had I been patient. You might be thinking, *He's really got a problem with impatience.*

The Bible says in James 1:4 (ERV), "If you let that patience work in you, the end result will be good. You will be mature and complete. You will be all that God wants you to be." This would have been a great verse to bring to mind during my ordeal. Instead, I allowed frustration to delay my forward motion.

I'm not alone; too many allow frustration to stop them. My charge to those individuals, as well as myself, is allow patience to mature you so that you can be all that God wants you to be.

Failure and Hopelessness

Many who suffer from depression would claim failures brought them to that sunken point in their lives. Furthermore, they saw no way to rise from the circumstance but felt hopeless and dejected.

Failure makes us feel as though we've messed up or missed it. It may even make us feel unworthy, like losers. However, Proverbs 24:16 (NIV) tells us, "Though the righteous fall seven times, they rise again...." This verse gives us hope because the reality is we're all going to stumble or mess up at various points in our lives.

God's people are not perfect, and we are not free from troubles or sin. We can, however, learn from our mistakes. Knowing what not to do and acting accordingly is how we rise. Honestly, I've learned more from my mistakes than I ever learned from my successes.

The Bible tells us that when believers fall into sin, we can find mercy with God when we repent. I'm not saying we have the liberty to sin, but I'm shedding light on a truth found in God's Word.

You may have made promises to your spouse, kids, or someone else and failed to keep your word. The enemy wants to make you feel like a failure, but I'm telling you that the key to overcoming that negative feeling is to accept the knowledge imparted to you by your hurts and failures and rise again.

Hank Aaron, Major League Baseball's greatest home run hitter, is recognized for hitting 755 home runs. But do you know that he struck out over 1,300 times? No one really talks about the strike-outs in his life; his fame is attributed to the home runs he made.

Many people don't try again after failure. They view it as fatal and final. Where it should be a moment in their lives, they view it as a monument or forever.

Evil Knievel, the great daredevil, was paid for his attempts, not his landings. David and Bathsheba lost a child but chose to try again and produced Solomon. You, too, can try again.

Here's what I know, great people, champions and heroes are human just like you and me. They strike out on occasion. Peter messed up; he denied the Lord. John Mark messed up when he forsook Paul on the mission field. And I think the greatest example of failure is found in the life of Samson. Samson made huge mistakes in his life with women, which cost him greatly. He lost his strength when his hair was cut. He was blinded and imprisoned. But eventually, he yielded to God's great purpose for his life, and he killed more Philistines just before he died than he had during his whole life.

The moral of the story is when you mess up, turn to God; don't give up. Thank God for 1 John 1:9 (ERV), which states, "But if we confess our sins, God will forgive us. We can trust God to do this. He always does what is right. He will make us clean from all the wrong things we have done."

SOLUTIONS FOR DEPRESSION

Take Charge

The Bible says that Jesus took upon Himself the nature of a man (Philippians 2:7). That is why He understands us. Jesus experienced a variety of emotions, but he never allowed His emotions to carry Him into sin. His emotions were always under control.

Although there are times when I'm tempted to lose control, the Bible says the Lord allows tests for our good, but never to encourage us to sin. The Bible tells us in 1 Corinthians 10:13 (KJV):

> There hath no temptation taken you but such as is common to man: but God is faithful, who will not suffer you to be tempted above that ye are able; but will with the temptation also make a way to escape, that ye may be able to bear it.

Staying closely connected to God and influenced by the Holy Spirit has given me the strength not to allow my feelings and emotions to control me. It's okay to be emotional if we handle our emotions like Jesus.

Choose Faith

The Bible says in 2 Corinthians 5:7 (NIV), "We live by faith, not by sight." There may be times when you feel like quitting, but a feeling is not a reason to quit. You will never mature in the things of God as long as you're an individual who is ruled by feelings.

When I was diagnosed with stage 4 cancer in early 2008, people often asked me, "How do you feel?" My response was always, "It doesn't matter how I feel. By Jesus' stripes, I'm healed." My outlook and my future were not based on how I felt.

One person might ask another, "Do you feel like going to church?" If they answer "no," they generally don't go to church because they're led by how they feel, not led by faith.

God's Presence

Another remedy is the presence of God. Elijah experienced it on the mountain of God. In 1 Kings 19:11-13, we read about the encounter.

> Then He [the Lord] said, 'Go out, and stand on the mountain before the Lord.' And behold, the Lord passed by, and a great and strong wind tore into the mountains and broke the rocks in pieces before the Lord, but the Lord was not in the wind; and after the wind an earthquake, but the Lord was not in the earthquake; and after the earthquake a fire, but the Lord was not in the fire; and after the fire a still small voice. So it was, when Elijah heard it, that he wrapped his face in his mantle and went out and stood in the entrance of the cave.

60

The wind, earthquake, and fire did not make Elijah cover his face and go out, but it was the still small voice.

Believers are impacted more so by the tender mercies of the Lord than by wrath. The mild voice of Jesus, who speaks from the cross, has the power to turn our hearts.

Elijah's depression left when he experienced God's presence on that mountain. He said goodbye to fear and allowed his faith to carry him through. He would no longer be robbed of his joy. He would never again be fooled into believing that God didn't have something better for him, or that the circumstances he was experiencing were too great for God to help, or that God didn't have a better future for him.

You, too, can experience God's presence as you yield to Jesus. He can break the depression and every weight you're carrying today.

In the story of Elijah, it says in verse 3 that Elijah left his servant. Hanging around and not leaving your healthy friends is another key to fighting depression. The tendency is to isolate, but we need associations. We need people to listen to us, console us, advise us, encourage us, and pray for us. So, find and build a dream team so that you don't battle alone.

ACT NOW

If you've been diagnosed with depression, ask and believe God for healing. Don't let another day pass without giving your situation to God because He has the miracle you need. He can heal you if you just believe. Whatever you're struggling with—

failures in your life, frustrations in your life, severe fatigue, or tremendous fear—give it to God in prayer, and have faith that He can liberate you.

Additionally, don't turn away from those who want to help. I encourage you to get involved with a support group—people taking action to break free from the bondage of depression. Seek advice from a professional Christian counselor or a self-help program that can lead you to victory over depression. Consider scheduling an appointment with an M.D. who can prescribe medication to help you through this season. The help you receive from others may be for a short time or an extended period, but know there's absolutely no shame in utilizing this recourse.

Consider helping someone who has challenges in his or her life, and you will likely see your situation in a different light.

Lastly, find a church that teaches the uncompromising Word of God.

Prayer

Father in Heaven, in the name of Jesus, I take authority over every form of depression that's been oppressing my mind. I bind and rebuke the stronghold and depressive spirits that want to control my mind, in the name of Jesus. No matter where it happened, no matter how it happened, I break the assignment against me now, in Jesus' name.

Father, I ask you to take the cares and concerns that overwhelm my life. Bring your peace that surpasses all understanding and release joy, peace, and laughter into my life. Depression, leave! I choose now to be free!

In Jesus' name. Amen.

Questions

If depression has ever crept into your life, how did you handle it, and what measures did you take to overcome it?

_____

_____

_____

_____

Have you ever found yourself in a situation similar to what Elijah experienced? If so, explain the circumstance and how God spoke to you.

_____

_____

_____

_____

We know that fear is not from God, but have you experienced fear that stopped you in your tracks? Explain:

_____

_____

_____

_____

Do you control your emotions, or do your emotions control you? What do you think you can do to overcome the emotional merry-go-round?

_____

_____

_____

_____

Additional Notes:

_____

_____

_____

_____

CHAPTER 3

DON'T BE TROUBLED

*Be strong and courageous. Do not be afraid or
terrified because of them, for the LORD your
God goes with you; He will never leave you nor
forsake you."*
—Deuteronomy 31:6 (NIV)

Not long ago, I was conducting research involving events that
took place during the decade I was born—the 1960s. My study
confirmed things I already knew—the '60s were tumultuous
years. Americans were greatly troubled as many protested and
demanded an end to the unfair treatment of African Americans,
an end to the war in Vietnam, and equality for women. Native
Americans brought attention to the gross injustice they
experienced concerning land appropriations, and migrant
farmworkers labored tirelessly to bring about change to their
work conditions.

The effects of the unsettling and troubling times of the '60s shaped the counterculture movement, which consisted primarily of young people who rejected many of the beliefs that were commonly held by society at large. As change began to take root, family values began to transform, and so did religious beliefs. What society didn't know at the time was how those changes would forever transform the American culture and the look of the traditional American family.

Many of the songwriters of the '60s expressed their views in their music. The young singer-songwriter Paul Simon wrote "Bridge Over Troubled Water." The following are the opening lines of the song:

When you're weary,
Feeling small,
When tears are in your eyes,
I will dry them all.

The song inevitably earned him several Grammy Awards, including Song of the Year.

Additionally, during that time, God intervened in a supernatural way. A grassroots, spiritual movement entered the scene with a mild explosion that revolutionized millions of lives. It was called "The Jesus People Movement," which, among other things, greatly influenced Christian music as well as Catholicism's charismatic movement.

Fast-forward to today, the young adult culture of the 21st Century with its wide range of uncertainties is quite similar to that of the '60s—many appear restless, unhappy, and dissatisfied with the status quo. Today, however, society is fighting different wars: war on terrorism, war on drugs, war on human trafficking, war on cyberspace, war on epidemics, and the fight for equality continues. In addition, the threat of nuclear bombs as well as social and political injustice is "breaking news" more often than not. The effects of these troubling times have produced many unsettled hearts.

You may conclude that we live in a troubled world that's getting worse every day. You may wonder if it's even possible to live in this world and not be troubled. Well, you can't stop trouble from happening, but you can control your reaction. The Bible says, "In the world you will have tribulation [trouble]; but be of good cheer, I have overcome the world" (John 16:33). Although we're living in troubling times, we don't have to be troubled about the trouble.

You might ask, "Is there hope? What can I do to bring change to my world?" The answer to these questions is found in 2 Chronicles 7:14:

> If My people who are called by My name will humble themselves, and pray and seek My face, and turn from their wicked ways, then I will hear from heaven, and will forgive their sin and heal their land.

As believers, we know that the only real and lasting change-maker for today and forever is Jesus Christ.

JESUS, OUR PROTECTOR

Jesus is the only true and proven defender of God's children, yet when trouble hits, sometimes we react in a way that resembles

69

distrust. I would say it's similar to the way a dog reacts when his property is threatened. When he feels challenged—maybe his bone is being removed from the yard—instead of a wagging tail, you hear a growl and are possibly bitten. It is an instinct for him to protect his turf.

Let me ask you a question. Have you lost the wag in your tail because you're losing control and are feeling troubled? If you answered "yes," then who are you relying on to protect your stuff today? Who's insuring your stuff and watching over it? What or who do you believe is protecting you?

Maybe you're trusting that your gifts or talents will keep you protected. Maybe you feel protected because of who's in office or you feel protected because you earn a paycheck. Perhaps some feel protected because they have an alarm system, a weapon under the pillow, or 24-inch biceps.

As followers of Christ and believers in God's Word, we can go to the Bible, which clearly points us in the right direction, and reveals everything we need to know about the One who provides our protection. Furthermore, we are to trust Him as the source of our strength and encouragement rather than the nightly news, which focuses primarily on the trouble.

John 14:1 (NIV) says, "Do not let your heart be troubled [distressed or agitated]. You believe in [adhere to, trust in, rely on] God; believe also in Me." These are Jesus' words. They're not the words of a therapist, guru, or counselor. When He said, "Do not...," He was not making a suggestion; it was a commandment. Our Heavenly Father knows what's best for us.

In this verse, we see the word "heart." The heart that Jesus is referring to isn't the muscle in your body that pumps blood through your veins. Jesus is talking about your mind and your emotions. He is telling you how to deal with the pressure of living in a troubled world. He's telling us not to allow our minds and emotions to become agitated, and not to become distressed. He's saying that we can trust Him to take care of it. And one thing is certain: Jesus would not tell us to do something unless it is possible.

We must grant ourselves permission to feel troubled. It can't happen without our consent. Do as Jesus commands, and don't allow yourself to become agitated or distressed.

CHOOSE TO BELIEVE

Not too long ago, I faced a distressing situation. I was praying and believing God for change to take place, and for a particular circumstance to get better in my personal life. My faith was strong and I was thanking God for the answer. I received a phone call one day, and the person on the line told me the situation was actually getting worse.

As soon as I heard what the individual said about the situation, my heart dropped. It felt heavy, and I began to feel troubled about what I had just heard. The enemy began to cast doubt, and pictures started to form in my mind of a downward spiral as if to say, *It's done, it's over, give it up.* Feelings of concern and discouragement began to overwhelm me. My perspective changed at that moment.

Just before the phone rang, I arrived home from work and was about ready to make a delicious salad with kale, arugula, fresh tomatoes, cucumber, soft feta goat cheese, and wild sockeye salmon. It was going to be amazing! I was going to sit down and enjoy that delicious salad, rest in front of the television for a bit, and then go back to work.

I had a plan, but after the phone call, I didn't feel like eating and I didn't feel like watching television. I was completely stunned by the news. It was as if disturbing thoughts were racing through my mind a thousand miles an hour and preventing me from focusing on anything. Honestly, nothing but the news I was given mattered.

In the midst of that troubling situation, I decided that I just needed a break. I went into my backyard and quieted my spirit. I began to pray very softly in the Spirit, and guess what? It didn't take hours for the atmosphere to change. There in my backyard, God gave me the peace I needed concerning the situation almost immediately. He said, "Nothing has changed. Trust the process and stay on the path."

That simple revelation from my Heavenly Father made all the difference. It altered my perspective to one of faith. I began to believe again that the promise He gave would indeed manifest in due time.

That simple revelation is something we should all take to heart. If you receive a promise that circumstances will be better, but sometime later, a word of trouble comes to you, I want you to trust that God will tell you that nothing has changed and to trust the process. Choose to believe that the promise will be fulfilled in due time.

The promise given to me by God well in advance of the phone call was, "I'm going to take care of this. It's going to be a favorable result." That day in my backyard, God reminded me to trust Him and believe His promise. It was like He was saying, *Now that you've heard something different, what makes you think that my promise has changed? I didn't tell you it would be a perfect road or that there wouldn't be obstacles and opposition. Where did you get the idea that's the way it would go down? Trust the process and stay on the path toward the destination and the promise.*

Let me share another example concerning trust. An activity that I truly enjoy is bike riding, and I normally ride with other guys. We usually ride the same familiar path every Saturday. We enter the trail, which is adjacent to a park, bike to the top, come down on another trail, and then head back to the area where we started.

Recently, I took a bike ride by myself. I started the same way I do when I ride with friends but along the way, I decided to take another route. Because I was so familiar with the area, I figured the trail would connect to the main path because it was actually the trail that we come back on when we ride as a group; I just entered it at a different point than usual.

While riding on the path, I became somewhat unsure that I was on the right path because the surrounding area seemed different. I began saying to myself, "I don't remember that tree." "I don't remember there being bumps here." "I don't remember the stump over there or that fence." All of a sudden, for just a moment, I was confused and wondered if I was on the road I was so familiar with.

I decided to stay on the path and tried to sort out my thoughts, and as I went a bit farther, I eventually came to where it connected to the main path as I had anticipated. At that moment, I knew I was on the right road.

In life, the familiar path is generally preferred. When God takes us in a different direction, all of a sudden, thoughts of doubt come. In those times, we may say, "Wait a minute; I'm not sure if I've ever been here before. I'm not sure I'm going in the right direction. I feel lost."

You've got to stay on the path; you've got to trust the process and realize that nothing has changed. You're going to arrive at your destination. Continue to move forward and don't become agitated by what appears to be unfamiliar. Just have faith. C.S. Lewis said, "There are far, far better things ahead than any we leave behind."

There's a great story in the book of Judges (chapter 6) about a man who received a word from God that totally went against what he thought to be true about his purpose. The man was Gideon, and he was called upon to save the children of Israel.

It was a troubling time for the children of Israel. They fell into rebellion and did what was "evil in the sight of the Lord" (Judges 6:1). As a consequence, they were given over to the Midianites.

In verse 12, we read, "The Angel of the Lord appeared to him

[Gideon], and said to him, 'The Lord is with you, you mighty man of valor!' Gideon's reply to the Angel of the Lord is found in Judges 6:13:

> Oh my lord, if the Lord is with us, why then has all this happened to us? And where are all His miracles which our fathers told us about, saying, 'Did not the Lord bring us up from Egypt?' But now the Lord has forsaken us and delivered us into the hands of the Midianites.

When you're experiencing chaos, or hearing troubling news, maybe your reaction should be like Gideon's. Cry out to God and ask, "Why is all this happening? Why is the enemy attacking me? Help me to understand." During a crisis, your mind is on overload and has you in a place of distress. Psalm 105:4 tells us, "Seek the Lord and His strength; seek His face evermore!"

God's response to Gideon was simple; He said (verse 14), "Go in this might of yours, and you shall save Israel from the hand of the Midianites. Have I not sent you?" Gideon's reply to God's response was (verse 15) , "Oh my Lord, how can I save Israel? Indeed my clan is the weakest in Manasseh, and I am the least in my father's house."

I can only imagine what Gideon thought when he received the word from God. He probably thought, *Lord, don't you know who you're talking to? Remember, I'm the weakest in the bunch. A mighty warrior I'm not.* God, however, saw something in Gideon that he didn't see in himself. God already knew that Gideon would be victorious in the battle. He just needed him to be a willing vessel.

The truth in this story is that God was merciful. With God's help, Gideon successfully delivered the people of Israel from the hand of the Midianites.

When trouble comes your way, believe that God will be there to deliver you as well. And if you receive a promise from God about your troubled marriage, troubled children, troubled job, or troubled health, stay focused and on the path. Deliverance will come.

TROUBLE AND DISTRACTIONS

There's a familiar story in the Bible about Jesus' visit to the home of Mary and Martha. I have read that story many times and preached multiple sermons that included that passage of scripture. I can relate to it, and I'm sure you can too.

The story reveals how quickly someone can become distracted, as was the case when I received that discouraging phone call. I was expecting a different outcome than the report I received.

I will use the story about Mary and Martha throughout the remaining pages to illustrate various points.

The Bible states in Luke 10:38-40:

> Now it happened as they went that He entered a certain village; and a certain woman named Martha welcomed Him into her house. And she had a sister called Mary, who also sat at Jesus' feet and heard His word.
>
> But Martha was distracted with much serving, and she

approached Him and said, 'Lord, do you not care that my sister has left me to serve alone? Therefore, tell her to help me.'

Jesus' response to Martha's comment began with Him stating her name twice.

Has anyone, maybe a parent, called your name two or more times to get your attention? As a child growing up, did your parent ever say your full name to get your attention? In those rare instances when your mom or dad said your full name as it appears on your birth certificate, you always knew there was a valid reason.

I can remember my wife calling out to our son Nate when he was little, and she always got his attention, and mine, as soon as she said, "Nathaniel Joshua Mesa, get over here now!" Immediately I would think that something serious was about to take place.

When you hear your name spoken twice, there's got to be a good reason, especially when it is the Lord talking. He may have said Martha's name a second time because she wasn't listening when He said it the first time. Maybe He had to repeat it to get her attention because she was distracted by what she thought was important. Jesus said, "Martha, Martha, you are worried and troubled about many things. But one thing is needed, and Mary has chosen that good part, which will not be taken away from her" (verses 41-42).

When Jesus arrived at their home that day, Martha probably smiled and greeted Him as she opened the door. She may have been excited; Jesus was going to be a guest in her house.

Now, I don't know if the conversation went down like this, but as Martha opened the door, I imagine her saying something like, *Oh hi, Jesus. How are you? Come on in. It's such an honor to have you in our house. I am so blessed with heaven's best because you're here today.* But notice the change in Martha's mood. She lost her joy when she was left alone to do the work.

Oftentimes, our mindsets quickly change when expectations aren't met. We start off trusting God, believing God, and having faith in God, but our attitudes change to worry and disappointment when expectations fall short. We stop celebrating, stop going to church, stop praying, and stop reading our Bibles.

Martha wasn't the only one to switch up on Jesus. Remember the people who lined the streets of Jerusalem as Jesus entered the city? They were yelling, "Hosanna" (Matthew 21:9) on Palm Sunday, but by Friday, they were shouting, "Let Him be crucified" (Matthew 27:22). Then there's Peter who said, "I will not deny you" (Matthew 26:35), and the next thing he knew, he denied the Lord just as Jesus told him (Matthew 26:69-75).

I don't know about you, but I don't want to be fickle, fragile, or flighty. If Jesus is Lord, then Jesus is Lord no matter what is going on in my life—good or bad, peaceful or challenging, fun or difficult.

The Bible tells us that Martha became distracted with much serving. People become distracted and lose focus because of what they do, see, and hear, especially if it's contrary to what they should be doing or what they should believe.

There are those who initially believe that by Jesus' stripes, they are healed of a sickness or disease. However, when they visit the doctor and are notified of the latest CAT scan, X-ray, or blood test, they become distracted by the results and disregard the promises of God and what they initially believed.

Another person may believe for restoration in his marriage, but when he hears his spouse speak the word "divorce," he's distracted by her words and allows doubt to creep in.

The same can be true of finances. God may reveal that He will bless an individual's life financially, more than He has ever blessed the person before. However, when an unexpected bill comes in the mail, he or she becomes distracted by the bill and loses focus on the promise.

Don't let a fragile, fickle, or flighty outlook creep in and distract you from the promise.

Let's take a look at another example in the Bible that deals with distractions. This time it involves Jesus' disciples. Matthew 14:22-32 states the following:

> Immediately Jesus made His disciples get into the boat and go before Him to the other side, while He sent the multitudes away. And when He had sent the multitudes away, He went up on the mountain by Himself to pray. Now when evening came, He was alone there. But the boat was now in the middle of the sea, tossed by the waves, for the wind was contrary.
>
> Now in the fourth watch of the night, Jesus went to

them, walking on the sea. And when the disciples saw Him walking on the sea, they were troubled, saying, 'It is a ghost!' And they cried out for fear. But immediately Jesus spoke to them, saying, 'Be of good cheer! It is I; do not be afraid.' And Peter answered Him and said, 'Lord, if it is You, command me to come to You on the water.' So He said, 'Come.' And when Peter had come down out of the boat, he walked on the water to go to Jesus. But when he saw that the wind was boisterous, he was afraid; and beginning to sink he cried out, saying, 'Lord, save me!' And immediately Jesus stretched out His hand and caught him, and said to him, 'O you of little faith, why did you doubt?' And when they got into the boat, the wind ceased.

When the disciples saw Jesus walking on water, they became afraid. They thought He was a ghost. Can you imagine? They were the same disciples who had been with Him since the beginning. They traveled with Him, ate with Him, and saw Him perform miracles, but when they saw Him walking on the sea, the Bible tells us (verse 26), "They cried out for fear." They should have been shouting and cheering Him on, saying, "Hey Jesus, we're over here. Wow! Look at Jesus; there's nothing He can't do." Instead, they were terrified.

Isn't that how many believers react? They can be in church singing and praising Jesus, but immediately they replace faith with fear if they receive troubling news.

The second thing I want to point out is Peter's reaction when he saw Jesus walking on water (verses 28-31).

Peter answered Him and said, 'Lord, if it is You, command me to come to You on the water.' So He said, 'Come.' And when Peter had come down out of the boat, he walked on the water to go to Jesus. But when he saw that the wind was boisterous, he was afraid; and beginning to sink, he cried out, saying, 'Lord, save me!' And immediately Jesus stretched out His hand and caught him, and said to him, 'O you of little faith, why did you doubt?'

Peter was doing so well; he was walking on water toward Jesus. So why did Peter begin to sink? Peter took his focus off of Jesus. He began to focus on the boisterous wind. Being distracted opened the door to fear and doubt, thereby affecting his ability to remain above the water.

Here is a lesson for all of us: When God gives us a word or a promise, and we know that we know it is from Him, we shouldn't allow the enemy to weigh us down with fear which affects our ability to remain afloat. Fear is a tactic he uses to steal the promises God gave us. Remember, our enemy is called a liar and a thief, and he tries to steal from us. Expect him to be himself. You be who God has called you to be—an overcomer.

Our confidence in God should never waver, for we know that the Lord holds true to His promises. The Bible states in 2 Thessalonians 3:3 (NIV), "But the Lord is faithful, and He will strengthen you and protect you from the evil one."

No matter how much our enemy, like the big bad wolf, will huff and puff and try to blow our houses down, it won't work as long as our faith and foundation are secure in Jesus. Choose not to fall for the enemy's lies, but choose to remain firm and fixed in what you believe.

To be troubled is to limit your grasp on the truths found in God's Word, which contains the promise of an abundant life, not a limited existence. A troubling situation can cripple the vision you have for your future. It has the potential to steal your dreams, hopes, and faith for a changed life. That leads me to a story found in Acts 3:2-4.

> And a certain man lame from his mother's womb was carried, whom they laid daily at the gate of the temple which is called Beautiful, to ask alms from those who entered the temple; who, seeing Peter and John about to go into the temple, asked for alms. And fixing his eyes on him, with John, Peter said, 'Look at us.'

Why do you think Peter told the lame man, "Look at us"? The fact that the man asked them for a gift made it evident that he saw them.

The passage goes on to say in verse 5, "So he gave them his attention...." That is what Peter was looking for; he wanted to make sure the man was focused on them and not distracted by other circumstances. When the man entirely directed his focus toward Peter and John, in expectation to receive something, the man received his miracle (verse 7).

Proverbs 4:25-26 (AMP) is a great scripture about focus.

> Let your eyes look directly ahead [toward the path of moral courage] and let your gaze be fixed straight in

front of you [toward the path of integrity]. Consider well and watch carefully the path of your feet, and all your ways will be steadfast and sure.

No matter the circumstance you're in or how long you've been there, hold fast to the word and your confession of faith because God will not disappoint you.

SHAKEN IN MIND

There's a commercial by Travelers Insurance Company that features a worrisome canine. You can look it up on YouTube. It's a funny advertisement for insurance that depicts real life.

The commercial is about a dog who is troubled about the possibility of someone stealing his bone. He can't rest or sleep until he finally gets insurance on his bone…Hmmm.

That worrisome canine was shaken in his mind like we sometimes get. We just have to remember we've got insurance; we're covered. Why be troubled when Jesus is our provider?

In the next example, I want you to notice how easy it is for a person to be distracted, as well as victimized, by those who come to deceive the body of Christ.

According to 2 Thessalonians 2:1-3, the Apostle Paul addressed believers who became troubled because of deceptions that were communicated concerning the return of Christ. The people seemed to be losing their faith about whether Jesus had returned.

They were allowing the persecutions of that day to influence and steal their faith, but Paul cautioned them, "Not to be soon shaken in mind or troubled, either by spirit or by word or by letter...." Evidently, he perceived that they were weak in their faith and vulnerable to deception by the enemy.

That is exactly what can happen to us if we're not strong in our faith. The enemy can send misleading messages that sound good but contain no truth. We must consistently declare that we will not allow any man or the enemy to distort or deceive us from the truth. The Bible tells us in Ephesians 5:6, "Let no one deceive you with empty words, for because of these things the wrath of God comes upon the sons of disobedience."

Make a conscious effort to fill your mind with true, just, pure, and lovely thoughts (Philippians 4:8). Say this: "I refuse to give in to fear." Declare 2 Timothy 1:7, "For God has not given us a spirit of fear, but of power, and of love and of a sound mind."

When it comes to the things of God, you and I can't effectively live out our God-given purpose if God doesn't have our attention. This is what the Bible tells us in Matthew 6:34 (MSG):

> Give your entire attention to what God is doing right now, and don't get worked up about what may or may not happen tomorrow. God will help you deal with whatever hard things come up when the time comes.

I love that truth. God doesn't want us to get worked up. People are working too hard at being troubled. People are working too hard at being fearful. People are working too hard at being anxious.

The Bible instructs us in Hebrews 12:1-2, "Run with endurance the race that is set before us, looking unto Jesus, the author and finisher of our faith, who for the joy that was set before Him endured the cross…." The Apostle Paul states in Philippians 3:14, "I press toward the goal for the prize of the upward call of God in Christ Jesus." You and I must focus on the prize associated with the promises of God and disregard the distractions.

When I was a little boy, although I was not diagnosed as such, I exhibited symptoms of Attention Deficit Disorder (ADD). ADD is included in a range of behavioral disorders, and it's recognized primarily in children. Symptoms include poor concentration, hyperactivity, and impulsivity.

The truth is I still struggle. Don't expect me to stay in one place too long, and don't try to have a long conversation with me because I will check out. My body will physically be present, but my mind will be on a bike ride, running, or recalling a scene from a movie because I will have mentally checked out.

It's important for me to go before the Lord in prayer consistently, and to read His Word. Doing so helps my mind to remain sharp and focused. I look at prayer and reading the Word of God as my therapy, my doctor's appointment, my drug of choice.

When our son Adam was a little boy, he was a very good athlete. He excelled at hockey and basketball. We tried putting him in baseball because he was such a good athlete. He didn't do so well in baseball because that sport is not as physical and does not involve as much constant movement as basketball and hockey. Baseball didn't capture his attention like the other sports.

Adam's position on the baseball field was in the outfield, so he had to stand there and wait for the ball to come to him. That often meant there was little for him to do for long periods.

At the start of an inning, Adam would have his glove propped and ready to catch a fly ball. But it wasn't long before his attention was diverted because he saw a butterfly, a dog, or one of his friends walking by. Anytime something like that would occur, Cindy and I would yell his name to get his attention, or his coach would shout, "Turn around!" Adam would refocus for a minute or so, but it wouldn't be long before he'd become distracted by something else.

As parents, we learned it was important for Adam to participate in a sport that he really enjoyed, and that also kept him engaged so that he could thrive in his athletic abilities. That also revealed his gifts and strengths to us.

Where do you thrive? Do you know your God-given purpose? That is an important question we all must consider. Maybe you think you don't have any talents or gifts, but God knows otherwise. The devil will try to steal your joy by telling you that you're not good at anything, but that's a lie.

It's time for you to take a leap of faith, step into your God-given gifting, and begin to thrive. There are a number of resources that can help you discover your purpose in the body of Christ. Popular assessments like Strength Finder, DISC Test, Enneagram, and Myers-Briggs are great resources. If you need help or would like to learn more, talk to the leadership at your church. They should be able to point you in the right direction.

HOW MUCH DOES GOD CARE?

During Martha's distraction, she questioned whether or not Jesus cared about her situation. She asked, "Lord, do you not care…?" Think about what Martha asked for a minute.

Would you ever have the audacity to look Jesus in the face and ask, "Do you care about what's going on in my life?" I'm sure the thought has crossed the minds of many people, especially when going through troubling situations.

The disciples asked Jesus a question similar to Martha's, according to Mark 4:38, when they found Him asleep in the stern of the boat during a violent storm. They asked, "Teacher, do you not care that we are perishing?" The intense wind and waves were realistic concerns, and the perceived danger caused their emotions to rise.

Knowing the end from the beginning, Jesus didn't demonstrate concern during the storm because He knew that at His word, the sea would obey. Jesus was always in control! What the disciples failed to realize was that the miracle worker was with them in the midst of the storm.

The Bible says in 1 Peter 5:7, "Cast all your cares on the Lord, for He cares for you." No one and nothing in this world wants to be burdened by the cares of others. Jesus is the only one who told us to give our cares to Him. He cares about your cares. He welcomes you to give Him your cares.

Throughout the Bible, God speaks over and over again about His love for us. From Genesis to Revelation, He reveals how much He cares for us. The following are just a few passages:

"How precious are your thoughts about me, O God. They cannot be numbered! I can't even count them; they outnumber the grains of sand! And when I wake up, you are still with me!"

—Psalm 139:17-18 (NLT)

"But the very hairs of your head are all numbered. Do not fear therefore; you are of more value than many sparrows."

—Luke 12:7

"The eyes of the Lord watch over those who do right, and His ears are open to their prayers."

—1 Peter 3:12 (NLT)

"I call on you, my God, for you will answer me; turn your ear to me and hear my prayer."

—Psalm 17:6 (NIV)

"This is the confidence we have in approaching God: that if we ask anything according to His will, He hears us."

—1 John 5:14 (NIV)

"You number my wanderings; Put my tears into Your bottle; Are they not in Your book?"

—Psalm 56:8

"Keep me as the apple of Your eye."

—Psalm 17:8

"Look at the birds of the air; they do not sow or reap or

store away in barns, and yet your heavenly Father feeds them. Are you not much more valuable than they?"

—Matthew 6:26 (NIV)

No matter what you're going through or what's troubling you; no matter who hurt you, who stole from you, or the losses you've experienced, believe and know that you serve a God who cares. If He didn't care, He wouldn't have gone to the cross. That alone shows you how much He cares for you.

You need to know today that no matter the pain, He has promised, "I will not leave you, nor forsake you" (Deuteronomy 31:6; Joshua 1:5, Hebrews 13:5). You may have failed, but it doesn't matter; He is committed to you.

Matthew 28:20 says, "Lo, I am with you always, even to the end of the age." Isaiah 43:2 says, "When you pass through the waters, I will be with you; and through the rivers, they shall not overflow you. When you walk through the fire, you shall not be burned, nor shall the flame scorch you." Psalm 23:4 reads, "Yea, though I walk through the valley of the shadow of death, I will fear no evil; for You are with me...."

God's love for us is not a conditional thing. He's with us in the good times and in the bad times. It has nothing to do with how holy or righteous we are, and it has nothing to do with whether or not we go to church. God's love for us is constant no matter what. God's commitment to us is stronger than the marriage vows we took when we said, "For better, for worse; for richer, for poorer; in sickness and health; till death do us part."

Just because things aren't going the way you thought, things look like they're getting worse, or something completely unexpected happens, that's no reason to feel unloved. Just because nothing is happening and you feel like God doesn't care, that doesn't make it true. Clear your mind of that thought and know, without a doubt, that He truly cares for you.

I remember when my boys were much younger, and Chuck E. Cheese and Toys R Us were a couple of their favorite places to go. On occasion, they would ask to go to one or the other, but Cindy and I would deny their request. A time or two, they would look at us and say, "You don't care...." I remember thinking, *Just because I don't take you to Chuck E. Cheese, you think I don't care? Just because I don't take you to Toys R Us, you think I don't care? Whose bed did you sleep in, and whose roof covered you today? What heater warmed you, or what air conditioner cooled you today? Whose food did you eat out of the refrigerator today? From whose closet did you get your clothes to dress yourself?*

Reflecting back on the statement my sons made makes me think about how God must feel when we question His love for us. He is the God who sent his only Son to save us; the God who provides the very air that we breathe, and the God who wakes us up each and every day. The moment something goes wrong, we question God's concern and love for us? Hmmm! Is our relationship with Jesus that shallow? Hmmm!

We're not random objects to Him. He knows each of us by name and knows the number of hairs on our heads. God truly is obsessed with us! He is always thinking about us. We cannot fully fathom how good He truly is to us and how much He genuinely cares.

Always remember that when trouble becomes your focus, it becomes a barrier between you and God. It hinders you from receiving His promises. Instead of focusing on His faithfulness, you're focusing on the seemingly insurmountable opposition.

Thinking back to the phone call, when trouble came into my situation, my initial outlook wasn't positive. But when I stepped outside and sought God's help, one particular scripture came to mind. I thought about Deuteronomy 6:10-12, which paints a clear picture of God's love.

> So it shall be, when the Lord your God brings you into the land of which He swore to your fathers, to Abraham, Isaac, and Jacob, to give you large and beautiful cities which you did not build, houses full of good things, which you did not fill, hewn-out wells which you did not dig, vineyards and olive trees which you did not plant—when you have eaten and are full—then beware, lest you forget the Lord who brought you out of the land of Egypt, from the house of bondage.

What do you have today that God didn't give you; that didn't come from His hand or His creation? Never forget what life was like before Christ.

When trouble comes, it distracts us, it separates us, it distances us, and it clouds our perception just like it did for Martha. She felt alone even though Jesus was just inches away.

When trouble comes, we have to be confident, knowing that our sovereign God sees and hears when we call on Him. Psalm 34:17-18 states, "The righteous cry out, and the LORD hears, and delivers them out of all their troubles. The LORD is near to those who have a broken heart, and saves such as have a contrite spirit."

If Jesus said, "Don't let your heart be troubled," it's an expression of His desire for your circumstances. Furthermore, it's a decision that you can control. It's a choice that you can make.

BE ON GUARD

The Bible states in 1 Peter 5:8 (MSG):

> Stay alert. The devil is poised to pounce, and would like nothing better than to catch you napping. Keep your guard up. You're not the only ones plunged into these hard times. It's the same with Christians all over the world. Keep a firm grip on the faith. The suffering won't last forever.

The Apostle Peter also said in 1 Peter 3:15 (NIV), "Always be prepared to give an answer to everyone who asks you to give the reason for the hope that you have. But do this with gentleness and respect."

In addition to the passages in 1 Peter, I encourage you to read the following verses, commit them to memory, and hide them in your heart so that you're never caught off guard during troubling times.

"Have mercy on me, my God, have mercy on me, for in you I take refuge. I will take refuge in the shadow of your wings until the disaster has passed."

— Psalm 57:1 (NIV)

"God is our refuge and strength, an ever-present help in trouble."

— Psalm 46:1 (NIV)

"The righteous person may have many troubles, but the LORD delivers him from them all."

— Psalm 34:19 (NIV)

"So do not fear, for I am with you; do not be dismayed, for I am your God. I will strengthen you and help you; I will uphold you with my righteous right hand."

— Isaiah 41:10 (NIV)

"Though I walk in the midst of trouble, you preserve my life. You stretch out your hand against the anger of my foes; with your right hand you save me."

— Psalm 138:7 (NIV)

No matter if you read the Word every day, pray every day, or go to church every day, as long as you choose to be troubled and agitated, the Word will not produce the power you need to defeat the enemy governing that negative emotion. The reason people go to church every week and leave unchanged is that they make their troubles larger than God.

The Bible states in Matthew 13:22, "Now he who received seed among the thorns is he who hears the word, and the cares of this world and the deceitfulness of riches choke the word, and he becomes unfruitful." The Bible says in Luke 21:34, "But take heed to yourselves, lest your hearts be weighed down with carousing, drunkenness, and cares of this life...."

What do you think the cares of this world and this life look like? How do they sound? What do they feel like? This might help you to identify them. I believe there's a distinct difference between concern about things and carrying cares. Concern is to exhibit an emotion or have a feeling about something, but it's momentary. Care is carrying the same emotion for an extended period of time. It remains and turns into a weight, a burden, a strong controlling sensation that dictates your actions.

When you're troubled by an avalanche of distress, worry, and doubt, the Word can give you strength to fight. God designed this weapon (His Word) to combat any and all schemes of the enemy. Hebrews 4:12 (NIV) states, "For the Word of God is alive and active. Sharper than any double-edged sword, it penetrates even to dividing soul and spirit, joints and marrow; it judges the thoughts and attitudes of the heart." To overcome the distress in your life, choose to use the Word.

In the early days of aviation, before planes were equipped with today's modern technology, pilots couldn't fly long distances for extended periods of time without landing to refuel. One day, a pilot took a long-distance trip and had to land partway through his journey to refuel before continuing his flight.

Shortly after takeoff, as the plane began to climb, the man heard something near the plane's pedals. There near his feet and the wiring, he saw a rat that had evidently entered the cockpit when he touched down to refuel. The rodent was gnawing away at the fuel line and wires. The pilot tried to kick the rat out of the way, but the critter was out of reach. He tried several times but was unsuccessful. The pilot began to panic as he thought, *If that rat cuts through a major line, I may lose control of the plane and crash.*

The pilot calmed himself and gathered his thoughts long enough to come up with an interesting solution. He thought to himself, *I'll pull back on the control wheel to elevate the plane, which will cause the oxygen level to drop and hopefully kill the rat.* Sure enough, he climbed in elevation and could see that the rat stopped gnawing as it struggled to breathe.

When trouble is gnawing at you, you've got to pull on the control wheel, and take that trouble into the presence of God. The Bible says it this way in Colossians 3:2: "Set your mind on things above, not on things on the earth."

Give your cares over to the Lord. Don't allow those cares to choke or eat away at the fruit that God wants to bring into your life. Matthew 6:25, 31, and 34 say the same thing: "Do not worry." Philippians 4:6 also tells us, "Be anxious for nothing... Let your requests be made known to God." Be anxious for nothing, not anything!

Take a moment right now to read the following sentences and insert your name in the blanks:

"_____ is worried over something that really

is nothing. _____ is worried over a nothing and is making it into a something."

It's like this: God was telling Martha, and God is telling you and me, "I got this! Don't be troubled over it because I've got it!" And here's what I know, if God says He's got this, then He's got it.

You may have had one or more of the following conversations with God about a situation in your life:

- "God, I owe a lot of money, and this trouble is weighing me down."

- "That person said a lot of things about me, God. What can I do?"

- "This is an impossibility I'm facing, God. What am I going to do?"

- "God, it's so bad that I feel as if I'm facing a death sentence."

Regardless of the conversations you have with God, the answer is always the same: He's got this! What do you think Jesus accomplished by hanging and dying on that cross? He hung on the cross to pay for the trouble that you're experiencing. He took the weight of mankind's sin upon Himself. He's got this!

There have been times when I've gone out to eat with people, and after we were done dining, I reached for the bill, but someone would say, "Oh, no, I've got this." I would ask, "Are you sure? It's a big bill. At least let me pay a portion of it." Before I could finish my sentence, the individual would say, "No, I've got this."

I would then respond with, "Okay, at least let me get the tip." Again, the response would be, "I got this!"

Why do we do the same with God? Why don't we give the burden to God instead of choosing to carry it? Is it because we doubt Him? Is it because we're not sure that God would say, "I got this!"?

Sometimes I play in golf tournaments; typically two-man or four-man scramble, best ball tournaments. That basically means we work together as a team. The way it works...we each line up and hit our balls, and wherever the best shot lands, we all get to continue from that spot. So if my friend hits his ball 300 yards down the middle of the fairway but my ball lands in the pond, I still get to take my next shot from where his ball landed—300 yards down the middle of the fairway.

The same is true with God. For all your failures, for all your mistakes, and all your quirks, God says, "I got this." You get to benefit from the work that someone else put in, and you avoid being penalized.

I did some research and discovered interesting information about worry.

- 40 percent of what people worry about is something that will never happen.

- 30 percent of what people worry about is in the past, which they can't change.

- 12 percent of what people worry about is health issues

that are really not health issues because they're not sick.

- 10 percent of what people worry about are insignificant, abandoned worries.

- Only 8 percent of what people really worry about is legitimate, which means 92 percent of what people worry about is not legit.

  (Retrieved from nightingale.com/articles/the-fog-of-worry)

When people worry, they aren't trusting God's promises or that God's got it.

Psalm 37:3 says, "Trust in the Lord, and do good; dwell in the land, and feed on His faithfulness." That's exactly what I began to do in my backyard that day after the phone call. I began to feed on God's faithfulness. Psalm 37:5 states, "Commit your way to the Lord, trust also in Him, and He shall bring it to pass."

The one thing you need to do about the trouble in your life is trust God. You may ask, "How do I trust God?" You trust God by getting in His presence (worship), His Word (Bible), talking to Him (prayer), and proclaiming His promises, and thanking Him in advance for the outcome (praise). Don't think about and dwell on the trouble.

Trusting God is an absolute necessity. It doesn't matter whether the sun is shining or it's raining; you need to trust God. You need to trust Him whether you've got a pocketful of money or no pockets. You need to trust God whether you've got a home or you're homeless. You need to trust God whether you're healthy or believing for healing to take place. You need to trust God whether you have a job or are unemployed. You need to trust God at the beginning of each circumstance, the middle, at the end, and well after each situation. Don't ever stop trusting Him! Psalm 9:10 states, "And those who know Your name will put their trust in You; for You, LORD, have not forsaken those who seek You."

Remember, you can trust God, for He never changes.

> "Jesus Christ is the same yesterday and today and forever."
> — Hebrews 13:8 (NIV)

Remember, you can trust God because of His unchangeable character.

> "God wanted to prove that his promise was true. He wanted to prove this to those who would get what he promised. He wanted them to understand clearly that his purposes never change. So God said something would happen, and he proved what he said by adding an oath. These two things cannot change: God cannot lie when he says something, and he cannot lie when he makes an oath."
> —Hebrews 6:17-18 (ERV)

Remember, you can trust God because of His good and perfect gifts.

> "Every good and perfect gift is from above, coming down from the Father of the heavenly lights, who does not change like shifting shadows."
> —James 1:17 (NIV)

Remember, you can trust God because of His unfailing love.

"Let the morning bring me word of your unfailing love, for I have put my trust in you. Show me the way I should go, for to you I entrust my life."

—Psalm 143:8 (NIV)

Remember, you can trust God for your salvation.

"For you have been born again, not of perishable seed, but of imperishable, through the living and enduring word of God."

—1 Peter 1:23 (NIV)

Whatever life has brought your way, do not be troubled. Continue your walk of faith because God will never fail you.

In closing, allow the simple words of an old song by Albert Goodson, "We've Come This Far by Faith," help you to remain strong in your faith.

We've come this far by faith,
Leaning on the Lord,
Trusting in His holy Word,
He's never failed us –yet.

Remember the story about the insurance company and the troubled, tired, worn down, beat down, sleepless dog that was worried that someone would steal his bone? Learn from him; it doesn't pay to worry.

Prayer

Father in Heaven, I thank you that you will never fail me. I pray against any troubling situation in my life today. I speak breakthrough and change to it. I speak deliverance to every circumstance. I speak a turnaround in my situation. I speak healing and salvation to this trouble. I speak wholeness and wellness to my spirit, soul, and body.

There is no situation where you cannot intervene and no problem that you cannot turn around. I thank you for calming my troubled heart as you turn my situation around.

In Jesus' name. Amen.

Questions

What troubles you the most? To whom and where do you go to get answers? Why?

_____

_____

_____

_____

Have you ever had a situation in your life that required total trust in God and you allowed Him to lead you? Explain.

_____

_____

_____

_____

Everyone gets distracted at one time or another. Share a time in your life when distractions diverted you from God's path. What was the outcome?

_____

_____

What do you do when trouble is gnawing at you? Give an example of when you were successful in the midst of trouble and when you weren't.

Additional Notes:

CHAPTER 4

LIFE WITHOUT STRIFE

Whoever loves a quarrel loves sin; whoever builds a high gate invites destruction. One whose heart is corrupt does not prosper; one whose tongue is perverse falls into trouble.
—Proverbs 17:19-20 (NIV)

Have you ever wondered why many people are sick? I'm not talking about the common cold or the flu. I'm talking about people who seem to be sick most of the time and don't have a clue as to why they're struggling with their health.

Although not necessarily the cause of all illnesses, I believe a key player is strife.

Emotions are a part of every-day life; however, researchers have found a link between positive emotions and good health. Emotions that make us smile and inspire us to do acts of kindness are good for us. Negative emotions, on the other hand, cause us to be withdrawn, sad, less thoughtful, unforgiving, bitter, and angry. If not controlled, negative emotions can influence us to harm ourselves or others.

Regarding strife, the Bible states the following in 2 Timothy 2:23-24 (AMP):

> But have nothing to do with foolish and ignorant speculations [useless disputes over unedifying, stupid controversies] since you know that they produce strife and give birth to quarrels. The servant of the Lord must not participate in quarrels, but must be kind to everyone [even-tempered, preserving peace, and he must be], skilled in teaching, patient, and tolerant when wronged.

As followers of Christ and servants of the Lord, we must realize that this verse is a command, not a suggestion.

Have you ever met someone who likes to argue? No matter what you say, it seems like they want to provoke you and get under your skin. I'm sure you have because these individuals exist within every race, creed, and culture. In fact, someone you know who fits the description probably just came to mind.

Argumentative people aren't looking for answers or direction. All they want to do is fuss and fight. For them, it's about divide and conquer, my way or the highway, and being highly critical and judgmental about anything and everything.

The Bible tells us to avoid foolish disputes since we know "they produce strife and give birth to quarrels." We are to be "patient and tolerant when wronged." Notice the word "tolerant." When people upset us, offend us, or get under our skin, we're expected not to engage in foolish conflicts. Simply put, we're expected to have thick skin. We must resist the urge to argue even if someone cusses us out. We are expected to be understanding and show love.

I know it's hard to resist the urge to retaliate, but scripture gives us clear instructions on how we are to treat those who upset us. Luke 6:27-28 (NIV) says, "But to you who are listening I say: Love your enemies, do good to those who hate you, bless those who curse you, pray for those who mistreat you."

A PICTURE OF STRIFE

As I mentioned, strife is destructive and causes many to suffer dis-ease. That may be a physical illness or state of mind.

Strife is clearly evident when rivalries exist, much like the rivalry between the New York Yankees and the Boston Red Sox. That rivalry initially started back in 1919 when Boston traded Babe Ruth to the Yankees. After the trade, the Yankees started winning big, and the Red Sox started to lose. From that point on, there was friction between the teams.

Now realize, the trade occurred 100 years ago, and Babe Ruth is long gone. Those still holding onto the rivalry need to let it go and just play ball!

Unfortunately, rivalries tend to draw the attention of the masses, and tension is maintained because interest is high. That is evident when it comes to reality television programs. With most, if not all, reality shows, strife between individuals improves ratings. Go figure! TV divorce court shows, heated talk shows, housewives' shows, and the like abound because that interests people.

Another picture of strife involves a boxing match that took place on April 6, 1893. Andy Bowen and Jack Burke stepped into a boxing ring; each hoped to emerge victoriously. The boxing match started at 9:00 p.m. but didn't end until after 4:00 a.m. the next morning; the two boxed 110 rounds. After seven hours and nineteen minutes, the fight was declared "no contest." In other words, no one won.

The definition of "no contest" is "an outcome in a combat sport where there is neither a winner nor a loser due to reasons outside of the combatants' control" *(The Free Dictionary by Farlex)*. Strife is pretty much the same. Individuals contend with one another, round after round, but in the end, no one can claim victory; it's "no contest."

There is no winner when it comes to strife; each party involved cannot have it their way.

NEGATIVE EMOTIONS AND DISEASE

Ohio University conducted a test within the Behavioral Medicine Research Department. It was administered to people who were full of strife and argumentative. The results showed that the test subjects' hormone levels rose significantly in a stress-induced environment which compromised their immune systems. It made their bodies less effective at fighting off disease.

It has also determined that various diseases such as diabetes, hypertension, and heart disease are associated with those who exhibit overly contentious characteristics. Many of those individuals believe they can continue to function well in the midst of strife and not suffer any adverse side effects. Nevertheless, studies show that the adverse effects of strife linger long after conflicts end, yet many fail to see the correlation between strife and their failing health.

The results of the studies revealed what occurs in the natural. How much more, though, is the spiritual life of a contentious person affected?

I'll share a personal story with you that will help to drive the point home. In the last two years, I twice suffered from a rash due to poison oak. I came in contact with the plant while riding my bike both times. I didn't know it right away, but about three days after each encounter, I started to itch. My arm became red, then blistery, and eventually would bleed. Both times I thought, *Where did this come from?* Both times, I didn't recognize the correlation between the blistery rash on my arm and the bike ride through the brush-filled terrain.

I've read that when you're affected by poison oak or poison ivy, it may take a few days before pain manifests, and it can take up to three weeks before the entire issue subsides.

Similar to the effects of poison oak, when your life is full of strife, sometimes you don't recognize the consequences of it for weeks, months, or even years. At some point, though, you find yourself on prescription medication due to an illness. You think to yourself, *How did this come about?* Could it be that years ago, you encountered the poison of strife that turned to bitterness and unforgiveness against someone who wronged you? Did you conceal it in your heart which eventually manifested in your physical body, compromising your immune system?

We are triune beings, and by avoiding strife, we can enjoy good health (spirit, soul, and body). Unfortunately, the world is full of strife. Not only does it exist in our homes but on our jobs, in politics, in our neighborhoods, and in our churches.

People experience strife in marriages because they fail to communicate. That has couples fighting about money, sex, kids, and a number of other things. People experience strife in relationships, which has friends fighting about who's going to win a game, who will outdo the other person, and who's in control. C.S. Lewis said, "Everyone says forgiveness is a lovely idea, until they have something to forgive."

Do you know how people dealt with strife and settled disagreements with one another in the 1700s and the early 1800s? Some would duel against one another.

When two people who strongly disagreed over something couldn't resolve their issue, they would arrange a set time and place to meet to engage in a pistol fight. They would stand back to back, with pistols in hand, and march out 24 feet. Then they would turn around and shoot their pistols at one another. It was a deadly way to settle disagreements yet common practice and legal.

The most famous duel in American history took place on July

11, 1804, between Alexander Hamilton and Aaron Burr—two politicians from New Jersey. Mr. Burr was the sitting Vice President of the United States, and Mr. Hamilton was the former Secretary of the Treasury. Hamilton and Burr didn't agree with each other on a matter, so they decided to settle it with a duel. Hamilton, who lost his son to a duel in 1801, pledged never to involve himself in such an event, but was provoked by Burr.

History tells us they met in a field, but Hamilton never intended to shoot Burr. He only wanted to scare him. After the two marched out 24 feet, Hamilton turned and fired his pistol. The bullet went over Burr's shoulder and hit a bush. Burr, unaware of Hamilton's true intentions, shot back and hit Hamilton in the belly. Hamilton died the next day as a result of the gunshot wound. *(Retrieved from en.wikipedia.org/wiki/Burr–Hamilton_duel)*

Just think, only 24 feet between them, and they couldn't resolve their differences which caused one to lose his life. That scene's reality was brought to light in the Broadway play *Hamilton* which I saw, and it was pretty awesome.

STRIFE WITH GOD AND SELF

Strife with someone who is contentious in nature is easy to recognize, but I believe there are situations involving strife that aren't as apparent, including striving with God and striving with self.

Have you ever heard someone say, "I'm mad at God," or say, "I don't want anything to do with God"? That is strife towards God. When I meet up with individuals like that, I want to ask,

"What went wrong; what did He do to you?"

Strife with God isn't something only non-believers experience. Christians also strive against God even though they may not say it or realize it. Many blame God for the adversities they experience, although He had nothing to do with it.

The Bible tells us that attacks are from the enemy, not God. 1 Peter 5:8 (NIV) says, "Be alert and of sober mind. Your enemy the devil prowls around like a roaring lion looking for someone to devour." This verse clearly tells us who is responsible for attacks we experience—it's the devil.

There are those who blame God (experience strife with God) although they chose to disobey His Word or disregard what He asked them to do. Their disobedience opened the door to adversities.

In the story of brothers Cain and Abel, we see that Cain was not only jealous of his brother; he also had strife with God. Why? He didn't do what God asked him to do with his offering, and he blamed God for the matter when he could have made the correction and done it right.

God is not our enemy but our Friend, Counselor, and our Savior, and He loves us. Knowing how much God loves us should cause us to stop and ask, "Why would I blame the one who loves me when I'm experiencing problems and disappointments? Why am I blaming the one who can restore my life? Why would I blame the one who is good and always gives good things?"

Think about it; why would you blame God for the unpleasant

circumstances that have occurred in your life when the apparent enemy is the devil who is seeking to devour you?

Realize that God's love for you is far greater than anyone could love you in a lifetime. There are many scriptures that reveal God's love for us in both the Old and New Testaments. Here are a few:

"How precious is your unfailing love, O God!"
—Psalm 36:7 (NLT)

"Dear friends, let us love one another, for love comes from God. Everyone who loves has been born of God and knows God."
—1 John 4:7 (NIV)

"And so we know and rely on the love God has for us. God is love. Whoever lives in love lives in God, and God in them."
—1 John 4:16 (NIV)

"We love because He first loved us."
—1 John 4:19 (NIV)

If you're guilty of striving with God, choose this day to end your grudge against Him and recognize that He truly loves you. His love for you is so real that He gave His only begotten Son that we may have an abundant life through Him and an eternal life with Him.

So what does strife with self look like? Well, when a person is striving with himself, he says things like, "I hate myself" or "I'm not good enough" or "I'm lousy" or "I'm good for nothing." These individuals generally struggle to forgive themselves. They find it difficult to let go of past hurts, shame, guilt, and condemnation.

Those who hate everything about themselves will generally hate the world they live in too. They tend to always find negativity in their environment and even the air they breathe. Their desire may even be to escape from themselves.

Hebrews 12:1-2 tells us, "Lay aside every weight and the sin which so easily ensnares us and let us run with endurance the race that is set before us, looking unto Jesus, the author and finisher of our faith...." T.F. Hodge said, "During moments of strife and 'dis-ease,' check your flow and redirect your focus to that which is naturally good."

Strife is not something you want to get comfortable with. It shouldn't be what you turn to as a means to help you cope with a matter. Nor should it be something you resort to and project toward others when you're really afraid. Strife is something you don't want in your life.

You may have heard of a "no-fly zone." The military sets up a no-fly zone to restrict aircraft from flying over certain areas. You and I need to protect our lives the same way. When strife tries to enter your airspace, enforce your no strife zone. Keep strife at a great distance.

ABRAM AND LOT

The story of Abram and Lot is a biblical account of strife that was brewing between two family members (an uncle and nephew). The devil always wants to destroy family and great relationships with strife.

The story begins in Genesis 12:1 (NIV): "The Lord had said to Abram, 'Go from your country, your people and your father's household to the land I will show you.'" Verse 4 states, "So Abram went, as the Lord had told him; and Lot went with him." The two men traveled together as herdsmen for a long time.

The story continues in Genesis 13:6-7 (NIV):

> But the land could not support them while they stayed together, for their possessions were so great that they were not able to stay together. And quarreling arose between Abram's herders and Lot's. The Canaanites and Perizzites were also living in the land at that time. So Abram said to Lot, 'Let's not have any quarreling between you and me, or between your herders and mine, for we are close relatives.'

The scriptures reveal that there was tension in the air and a major decision had to be made to maintain peace. Within this story are great teaching points that I will expound on as we continue the chapter.

The first thing you should take note of is that strife can be contagious. Think about that; another person's strife can creep into your life. Someone can share information about someone or something, and suddenly you feel animosity towards that person because of what you were told, not something you experienced.

Abram and Lot's relationship began to show signs of strife when the herdsmen began to bicker with one another. When Abram got wind of the dispute, he nipped it in the bud and came up with an amicable resolution. Abram spoke directly to Lot about the issue. He didn't allow strife to take root. Abram said (Genesis 13:9), "Is not the whole land before you? Let's part company. If you go to the left, I'll go to the right; if you go to the right, I'll go to the left."

In the end, the decision took each man on separate paths. Lot chose the fertile land; the path of Sodom, and Abram chose a less fertile land; a path less traveled. Lot eventually lost his possessions, and Abram gained blessing and honor. Abram was confident in what he knew—as long as he had God, God would bless him wherever he went.

There are times when difficult choices have to be made, and you just have to let go and move on. It may feel like you're losing the battle because you give in or you take the high road, but as believers, we are to seek peace at all cost.

Abram refused to get into a ruffle with Lot over the situation between the herdsmen. His decision opened the door for God to release an abundant blessing to him. In verses 14-15 of the same chapter, the Lord said to Abram, "Look around from where you are, to the north and south, to the east and west. All the land that you see I will give to you and your offspring forever."

By separating from Lot and the strife between the herdsmen, God began to reveal Abram's future and His will for him.

What else can we learn from this story and apply when we

encounter strife? Something to take note of is that Abram went to Lot, and when there is strife looming in the air, someone has to take the first step toward resolution. Taking the initiative means you arrange a meeting by picking up the phone or personally approaching the person with whom you have strife.

Strife will never be resolved if the individuals involved are at the same level of maturity and refuse to change; that's not how it works. It takes a bigger person to take the first step. Taking the first step isn't always easy, and if you choose to wait for the other person, you may have to wait forever.

Why not take charge by taking the first step to resolve the strife. There's an old saying, "There can be no resolution in a matter until someone has the courage to confront." Someone has to be Abram in the relationship because there are *a lot* of Lots.

ESTABLISH BOUNDARIES

When our boys were young, we made a rule in our home; we didn't allow strife. Like any other couple, my wife and I didn't always agree, but we would never argue in front of the boys. We made a promise to each other that we would not allow it to occur. Generally, we'd wait until evening to discuss our disagreements. However, there were times when we'd say, "Excuse us, guys," and the two of us would walk into another room and settle our differences behind closed doors. We never wanted them to hear us bickering because the consequences can be great.

Parents displaying their anger toward one another in front of their children can be emotionally damaging to the children. That's why going through a divorce is one of the most difficult times for a family. It's important to note that the way a divorce is handled will impact the children involved, which can mess them up.

No matter what one parent has done to the other parent, parents should not say things like, "Your no-good daddy (or momma)," because terms like that can be detrimental when communicating with children. A parent would never think of placing a bottle of Jack Daniels in their child's hand and begin drinking with him when he's five years old because that would hurt him. Negative words about a child's mom or dad can be just as harmful. Scientists and medical research tell us that children can grow up with an identity crisis, insecurity, and fear because of what they hear their parents say.

If our boys disagreed with one another, we also had a rule that there would be no fighting. I'd say, "You're not going to act like that. Don't put your hands on your brother." We taught them how to talk through their differences. We'd often make them resolve their issues in front of us and apologize because we didn't want strife in our home.

We also confronted them if they slammed the door to their room in anger. I'd say, "Wait a minute. You don't slam doors on me. This isn't your house, so I'm walking in."

When we were in public with our boys and they became upset and tried to throw a tantrum, we didn't embarrass them or call them out in the mall or the grocery store. We never humiliated them. Instead, I'd look eye to eye with them and say, "We do not react that way. Just because you are not going to get what you want, that doesn't mean you're going to throw a fit on this floor. Haven't mommy and daddy been good to you? Look at all the other stuff you have. We don't always get everything we want."

We established rules early with our children, and I encourage all parents to do the same because it can be much harder when they're older.

As the husband and father in my home, I've tried to be the initiator when dealing with strife like Abram. I've always tried to use wise judgment, and I wish I could say I've always been quick to initiate, but sometimes I exhibited pride. In my pride, I would tell myself, "I ain't talking to her. I don't even want to be around her." However, with God as my witness, in more than 30 years of marriage, I've never allowed the dispute to go on more than a day. Instead, I would go to Cindy and say, "I apologize; I'm sorry. Let's talk about it and see how we can resolve this issue." By taking that first step, I opened the door to reconciliation.

You might say, "Brother, that's not fair." I didn't always think it was fair either, but sometimes you have to take the first step. This principle doesn't only apply to marriage, but it can be utilized in any relationship.

Even though Abram, as the patriarch of the family, had the authority to take the best land, Abram allowed Lot to have the choice land to avoid conflict. The Bible says in Proverbs 20:3 (NIV), "It is to one's honor to avoid strife, but every fool is quick to quarrel." An honorable man knows how to end the striving, and Abram was an honorable man. He took steps to stop the strife before it got out of hand. Additionally, he had a very close relationship with God, which was worth more to him than a piece of property.

Abram was more mature and wiser; however, Lot was foolish and didn't consider what his decision would one day cost him. When Abram said, "Please part from me; if you go left, I will go right, and if you go right, I will go left (verse 9), " Lot could have said, "Oh no, Uncle Abram, you choose first the land you prefer. You're my elder. Without you, I wouldn't be here today." Instead, Lot chose first. His attitude said, "Get out of my way; I'm going to get me mine."

In Galatians 5:16, 19-21 (ERV), we read the following:

> So I tell you, live the way the Spirit leads you. Then you will not do the evil things your sinful self wants. The wrong things the sinful self does are clear: committing sexual sin, being morally bad, doing all kinds of shameful things, worshiping false gods, taking part in witchcraft, hating people, causing trouble, being jealous, angry or selfish, causing people to argue and divide into separate groups, being filled with envy, getting drunk, having wild parties, and doing other things like this.

Many people will stand against sexual immorality, idolatry, sorcery, and other blatant forms of sin. They recognize them as wrong and want no part of them. Yet when strife, anger, and dissension come into their lives, they turn a blind eye and fail to see the iniquity. Maybe in their minds they are justifiable because some consider these respectable sins.

God calls strife a work of the flesh, and it's a sign of immaturity and carnality. Paul says in 1 Corinthians 3:3 (ERV), "You are jealous of each other, and you are always arguing with each other. This shows that you are still following your own selfish desires. You are acting like ordinary people of the world."

THE GREAT DIVIDER

The next point I want you to take note of is the statement Abram made when he said, "Let there be no strife between us." Abram recognized that peace and unity were essential.

Paul wrote in Ephesians 4:3 (NIV), "Make every effort to keep the unity of the Spirit through the bond of peace." In Romans 12:18 (NIV), he wrote, "If possible, so far as it depends on you, be at peace with everyone." Jesus said in Matthew 5:9 (NIV), "Blessed are the peacemakers, for they will be called children of God."

The nature of strife is to divide. Strife always wants to get in between good, godly, put-together-by-God relationships.

Satan is the great divider, the instigator, and the maker of strife. He hates unity because unity brings God's power and God's peace into people's lives along with God's blessings.

The nature of Satan is strife. Consider what the Bible tells us about him. God created him but he rebelled against God, and he was so influential that he took one-third of the angels. Why? Read Isaiah 14:13-14 and take note of his words: "I will ascend..., I will exalt..., I will sit..., I will be like the Most High."

How many times have you walked into a room and without hearing anyone speak, you felt the negative energy of strife? The reason you feel it is because it's a spirit.

Just as peace is a spirit, so is strife, and strife destroys. Wherever strife exists, so does the presence of the enemy. Because the enemy hates unity, he will try to come between you and someone to drive a wedge between the two of you. Be on guard and watch for signs of strife in your relationships because the enemy is subtle.

Let's say you have a best friend to whom you sent a text which stated, "I need you right now!" Your friend, however, didn't text back. What kind of thoughts and feelings would begin to rise in you?

For some, you're ready to kick your friend to the curb even if you've known her for 30 years. You're upset because you're not getting the timely response you desire. You don't know if your friend's phone died, if she had to take a parent to the hospital, or if she is intentionally ignoring you.

Where does that feeling of outrage come from? It comes from the flesh; it comes from the enemy whose intention is to divide.

When there was contention between Lot and Abram, the Bible tells us that the Canaanites and the Perizzites dwelt in the land. That means they were likely aware of what was going on between Abram and Lot. Similarly, someone is probably aware of the strife you have with someone, which affects your witness. People tend to remember the negativity that comes out of your mouth more than the positive things you say.

Maybe you had a disagreement or experienced strife with a neighbor. It's very difficult to lead your neighbor to the Lord or invite them to church when you're at odds with them. Furthermore, other people like your children, who are innocent bystanders, can be affected by or even emulate your behavior.

Another story involving strife between family members is found in Numbers 12 (ERV). It took place between three siblings: Moses, Aaron, and Miriam. For a time, they were like The Three Musketeers—a triple-team that was powerful when they were united.

We see in verse 1 how strife entered the relationship—Aaron and Miriam had an issue with who Moses chose to marry. Then in verse 2, we read, "Miriam and Aaron began to talk against Moses. They said to themselves, 'Moses is not the only one the Lord has used to speak to the people. He has also spoken through us!'"

According to the end of the verse, the Lord heard Aaron and Miriam murmuring and complaining. The spirit of jealousy had entered their hearts, and God confronted them.

> When I speak to him, I talk face to face with him. I don't use stories with hidden meanings—I show him clearly what I want him to know. And Moses can look at the

very image of the Lord. So why were you brave enough
to speak against my servant Moses?

—Numbers 12:8

We learn in Luke 22:24 (NIV) that there was strife among
Jesus' disciples. They were arguing about who was the greatest
among them; in other words, who Jesus considered to be His
number-one man. In verse 26, Jesus said, "The greatest among
you should be like the youngest, and the one who rules, like the
one who serves." He nullified their dispute by explaining what
greatness entails.

Jacob and Esau were two brothers who fought over an inheritance.
Only after years of an estranged relationship and strife between
the two brothers did Jacob and Esau finally reconcile with one
another.

Remember, although the enemy comes to divide, it's up to us
to decide that the conflict is not worth the loss. We've got to
deal with ourselves, or we've got to talk it through with others
because our relationships are too important. It's up to us to
decide whether or not we're going to allow the enemy to destroy
the relationships we've established.

In the story of Joseph, we learn that he was the youngest and
most favored of Jacob's twelve sons. Jacob made the mistake
of demonstrating more affection towards Joseph, which created
intense jealousy between the brothers. The jealousy and envy
rose to the degree that the brothers came together and plotted to
kill him one day. But instead of killing him, they sold him into
slavery and told their father Jacob that he had been killed.

The brothers didn't know then that there would come a time when Joseph would be second in command in Egypt. The brothers who had done him wrong would have to go before him to ask for food to survive during a time of famine.

Years later, when his brothers came to Egypt for food, Joseph had the power to enslave them, kill them, or be merciful to them. That day, Joseph showed compassion toward his brothers and was eventually reunited with his father Jacob (Genesis 46:28-34).

I can't help but think that Joseph may have remembered the story his father told him about his Grandpa Abram and Cousin Lot. Did Joseph show mercy towards his brothers because of Abram's decision to choose relationship over strife?

Jealousy is often recognized as coveting what someone else has or a position that someone holds. We learn from the aforementioned examples that there is no benefit in being jealous of one another. God is not going to respect one person over another. We are all God's children and have unique callings on our lives. We should work together for the good of the family, the church, and our neighbors because a house divided cannot stand, and a little bit of jealousy can do a lot of harm to all parties involved.

Whether it's the story of Abram and Lot, Moses and his siblings, Jesus' disciples, Jacob and Esau, or Joseph and his brothers, I can't help but wonder if the devil laughed at them just like he laughs at us when we're fighting against each other instead of against him. John 10:10 (NIV) says, "The thief comes only to steal and kill and destroy; I [Jesus] have come that they may have life, and have it to the full."

AVOID STRIFE - CHOOSE UNITY

There's a famous hockey player, Stan Makita, who is known for fighting during hockey games. When hockey players fight, they're penalized, which requires that they sit out of the game for a period of time. Stan Makita's young daughter said something to him that was very profound. She asked, "Daddy, how can you score goals if you're always in the penalty box?"

I present you with this question: How can you score against the enemy and do great things in the kingdom of God when you're always in strife's penalty box?

My battle with cancer years ago was tough, and, for a season, every day was emotionally draining. It was so draining that if I had allowed it, my condition could have altered my personality.

I can tell you from personal experience, don't allow a condition or situation to alter your personality, and don't use a condition or situation as an excuse. Going through tough times doesn't grant you the right to have a negative attitude.

On one of my not-so-good days, I went to get gas. At that gas station, there were lots of pumps, which were all occupied with cars. In addition, other cars were approaching the pumps from different directions. Basically, it was every man for himself!

As I waited, I saw a car leave which opened a slot at a pump, so I went for it. I was driving a full-size truck and couldn't easily maneuver around the cars, so I had to back-up into the space. I pulled forward a bit to better position my truck, and as I began to back in, a small car came in and took the slot I was trying to take. I watched it through my rear-view mirror, and I was shocked!

I put my truck in park, rolled down the window, and said to the driver of that car, "Sir, I was about to back up to that pump."

He said, "I didn't see you."

I replied, "You probably didn't. Because my truck is so big, I had to move forward first before I could back in."

The man looked at me and asked, "Well, what are you going to do about it?"

He was challenging me right there at the gas station. It was like a wrestling match showdown that you see on TV.

I opened the door of my truck and got out. Then I said, "I was here first, and if you don't get this car out of my way, I'm going to back my truck in and run over it!"

I normally have a very high tolerance for situations like that, but because of the season I was in, I was vulnerable. There I was, a senior pastor, involving myself in a conflict I could have easily avoided by remaining in my truck and waiting for a different pump that would soon be available. I know…pray for me.

During another incident, I was stopped at a red light. I looked to the left and then the right and saw an old truck with landscaping tools in the back rolling up between the lane I was in and the curb. I thought, *He's got to stop.* When the light turned green, all of a sudden, the driver cut in front of me. I didn't react; I just continued driving.

When I realized his vehicle didn't have enough power to drive the speed limit up the hill we were on, I zoomed around him. I didn't look at him or say anything.

As I continued, I noticed him in my rear-view mirror, and I could tell he was angry and obviously trying to catch me. I said to myself, "Oh, no you aren't." I pressed lightly on the brakes to slow down a bit. He was approaching fast, so I moved to the left to allow him room on the right.

The driver of the truck pulled up alongside my car, so I rolled the window down and said, "What's up?"

The guy replied, "Who do you think you are…cutting in front of me in your big old fancy car? Why don't you pull off the road?"

"I'm pulling off the road right now," I replied. "We're going to settle this."

We stopped our vehicles, and when he got out of his car, he was holding a pipe. I said, "You need the pipe? I don't need a pipe. I've got two pipes right here, buddy," pointing to my biceps.

In that moment, I couldn't say to that guy, "I'm the pastor of Abundant Living Family Church. If you need prayer, I would love to pray for you." Unfortunately, my witness went out the door when I allowed the situation to bring out the worst in me. I know…pray for me!

When I was diagnosed with cancer, I saw a doctor who said, "Here are the things I want you to eliminate from your diet because cancer thrives on these things." The first thing he mentioned was caffeine. I said, "Oooh, my coffee; I love my coffee!" Next, he mentioned refined sugar, and I said, "Oooh, cakes and ice cream." Then he told me that cancer thrives on white flour. Of course, I thought of all the pasta and pizza that I would have to give up. The doctor informed me that if I didn't eliminate those things from my diet, I would be feeding the cancer. I had to stop feeding it.

Do you know what feeds strife? Gossip, being a busybody, and offense feed strife. Anger, impatience, unresolved issues of the past, and daddy issues feed strife.

Don't allow anyone to bring gossip to you about someone else. And don't be the person who is initiating the gossip. The Bible says in James 3:16 (ERV), "Where there is jealousy and selfishness, there will be confusion and every kind of evil." The Bible says in Proverbs 20:19 (NIV), "A gossip betrays a confidence; so avoid anyone who talks too much."

I'm amazed at how many people talk about other people, but I'm also amazed at how many people will let others gossip to them. If someone comes to me trying to gossip about someone, I'm going to shut the door on the conversation and say, "Does it say 'waste management' on my forehead? Don't be coming and dumping all that garbage on me. I am not in the waste management business." Basically, you have to put gossipers in their place, or it's never going to stop.

Looking again at the relationship between Abram and Lot, we

should recognize that strife yields to love. Abram was yielding to the love he had for his nephew Lot when he said, "You go to the left, and I'll go to the right, or you can go right, then I'll go to the left." Abram wasn't trying to hold his ground like I was at the gas station or on the side of the road. Abram wasn't saying, "I'm right; you're wrong." He was yielding, and through that, he prevailed over the strife that was brewing.

Strife cannot stick to you if you operate in love and peace, and strife will not last long if you strive for unity.

The following are additional scriptures that can help us overcome strife:

> "Most important of all, love each other deeply, because love makes you willing to forgive many sins."
>
> —1 Peter 4:8 (ERV)

> "God, you give true peace to people who depend on you, to those who trust in you."
>
> —Isaiah 26:3 (ERV)

> "Behold, how good and how pleasant it is for brethren to dwell together in unity!"
>
> —Psalm 133:1 (NIV)

One meaning for the word "pleasant" is attractive. You are attractive to God when you choose to be a person of unity. Verse 3 of that Psalm says, "In that unity is where I command blessings."

RECOGNIZE THE SIGNS

To overcome strife, you have to cooperate, and sometimes you have to compromise. It's also important to communicate and listen.

I enjoy bike riding. When I first started riding my bike in the rain, I would just put on a regular jacket. Do you know what would happen when I wore that jacket in the rain? The rain would soak through my jacket, and I'd become drenched.

I soon learned from my mistakes and looked for a jacket that was water-resistant and found one. I thought, *This is perfect.* The next day, I put the jacket on and went riding, and it began to rain. I didn't realize then that water-resistant doesn't mean waterproof. The longer I rode and stayed in the rain, the less resistant the jacket became, and by the end of the ride, I was drenched.

Eventually, I asked someone more knowledgeable about biking gear, and I was told to buy a jacket with polyurethane. I learned that polyurethane is woven into the fabric, making it waterproof so that no matter how much it rains and how long I ride, the rain won't soak through.

Taking the lesson I learned about biking gear and applying it to this topic, here's my tip for you. Learn from your mistakes! Don't continue to do the same thing expecting different results. That's not what a person of sound mind would do. Also, if you don't know how to change, seek guidance from a professional or credible source. Furthermore, consider that as long as you wear love and peace, and weave unity into the fiber of who you are, strife cannot soak through.

You can eliminate strife from your life. That's what Abram taught us by his example. He said, "Let's separate..." Everyone has a button that can be pushed to cause strife. We have to avoid pettiness, we can't overreact, can't be overly sensitive, and we have to avoid people who are.

Strife wants to rob you of the blessing that God has for you, which comes as a result of your obedience. Oftentimes, when God is about ready to use you, bless you, and promote you, strife will start to rise because the enemy wants to steal the blessing.

The enemy is always scheming; he tries to attack me with strife generally in the same instances. When I'm about ready to preach is one instance, and that's because he recognizes that God is about to use me. The other is when I come down from the pulpit. That's the way the enemy operates. He's ruthless, and he'll do anything to steal someone's testimony.

We should pray daily and ask God to give us wisdom and strength to avoid strife. Ephesians 4:29 (NIV) says, "Do not let any unwholesome talk come out of your mouths, but only what is helpful for building others up according to their needs, that it may benefit those who listen."

Let's not grieve the Holy Spirit and lose our joy and peace. Nehemiah 8:10 (NIV) says, "The joy of the Lord is your strength." Therefore, to complain and argue can actually weaken or cripple us, rendering us ineffective in the body of Christ.

As I conclude, I want you to consider this question: What price are you willing to pay for peace? Is it peace at any price, even if you're innocent in the situation? We should all be willing to pay the price Abram paid to bring about peace in our families, churches, and communities. We should choose peace by restating Abram's words, "Let there be no strife between you and me."

Taking the initiative to resolve an issue you have with someone doesn't mean you lost and they won. Instead, you're the one with the *courage* to confront.

There is a proper way and time to deal with negative behavior, but ignoring it is not a solution. If you don't feel comfortable taking charge, consider taking your eyes off your *Lot* and putting them on God. Say, "What I'm doing is as unto the Lord who has done so much for me." Think about how healthy and blessed you'll be by not allowing strife to remain in your heart. You'll wipe out problems that have the potential to cause dis-ease in your future.

Take a moment to give God all the strife in your life. Whether it's toward God, others, or self, give it to God today. If you want to live without strife, lay it all down right now and give it to God. If you don't know what to say, I have included a prayer to help you. Read it aloud and mean it with all your heart.

Prayer

Heavenly Father, today I give You all the strife and bitterness that's in my life. All the hostility, I give it to You. The strife that I have with You, the strife that I have with myself, and the strife that I have with others, I give it all to You.

I release your love in my heart. I release your peace in my life, and I accept the unity that only You can bring. I choose to be the Abram in my relationships. I choose not to be the Lot. It doesn't matter what was said. It doesn't matter what was done. I choose to look at how good You have been to me, God. I'm not going to hold this strife in me any longer because it's only making me sick and tearing me up on the inside. I now give it all to You, Lord. Thank You for removing it.

In Jesus' name. Amen

Questions

Strife can weaken the immune system. Have you experienced strife in your life that affected your health? What were the effects and the end result?

_____

_____

_____

_____

Has there ever been a time in your life when you had to do as Abram did with Lot and separate from someone? Explain.

_____

_____

_____

_____

Who is at the helm when it comes to strife in your life? Give an example of when strife arose and how you dealt with it.

_____

_____

_____

_____

What are steps you can take to eliminate strife from your life?

_____

_____

_____

_____

Additional Notes:

_____

_____

_____

_____

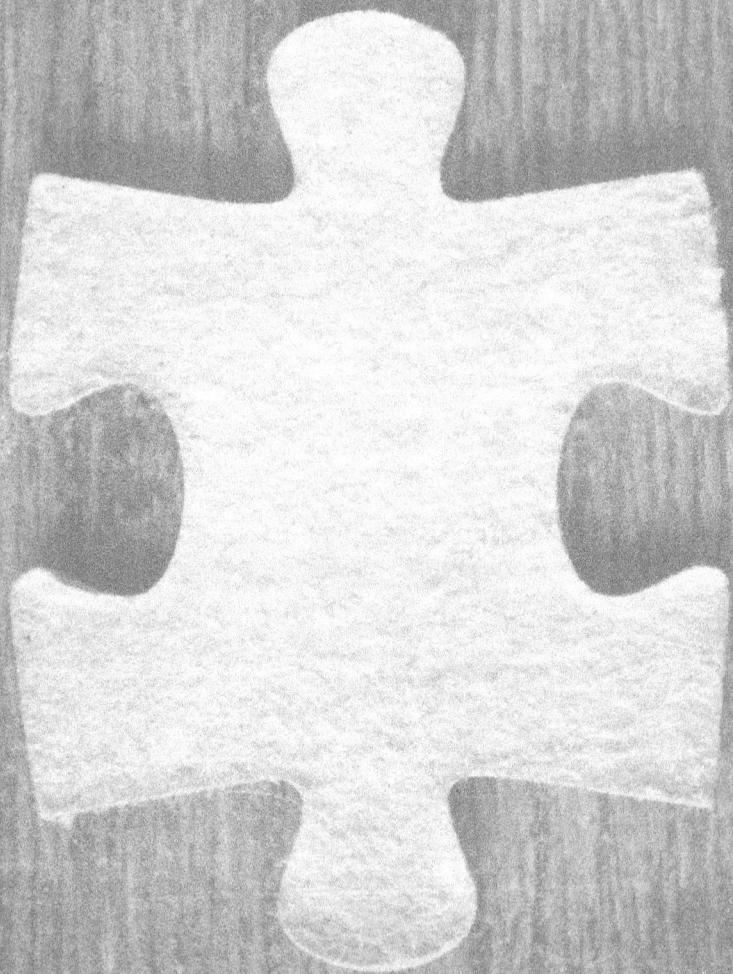

CHAPTER 5

WHAT DOES NEGATIVITY LOOK LIKE?

Finally, brothers and sisters, whatever is true, whatever is noble, whatever is right, whatever is pure, whatever is lovely, whatever is admirable— if anything is excellent or praiseworthy—think about such things. Whatever you have learned or received or heard from me or seen in me—put it into practice. And the God of peace will be with you.

—Philippians 4:8-9 (NIV)

When you look at your life, in general, do you see it as a glass that is half full (good, hopeful) or as a glass that is half empty (not so good, less hopeful)? An optimist sees his or her life as a glass that is half full, while a pessimist sees it as half empty. Which one best describes you?

I heard an interesting tale involving twin boys, which describes the difference between an optimist and a pessimist. Although the children were twins, the brothers were very dissimilar. Because of their diverse personalities, the parents took them to a therapist to figure out how their twins could be so different. One of the boys was very positive about life. The other had a negative outlook on life. They were complete opposites. The therapist put the twins in two separate rooms and watched their behavior in an adjacent room through a one-way mirror.

The pessimistic boy was placed in a room filled with toys. After a few moments, he began complaining about the toys. He made comments like, "I don't like the color of these toys." "They'll probably break." "These toys are boring." The pessimistic boy didn't realize that he was surrounded by the latest and most popular toys that other kids his age enjoyed playing with. He, however, found reason to complain about every one of them.

The optimistic twin was placed in a room filled with manure. The therapist and the parents watched as the boy used his hands to shovel quickly through the manure. The therapist became very curious about his behavior, so he opened the door and asked the boy, "Son, what are you looking for? Why are you shoveling through the manure, and why are you moving through it so quickly?"

The optimistic boy answered, "If there's manure in here, there's got to be a pony here somewhere."

Some believe that interactions within the twin's environment affected the development of their diverse personalities. The reason being, when we are born, we enter the world pure. There are no destructive emotions yet within us.

We're not born with negativity, jealousy, envy, pride, or hatred. These emotions are introduced to us as we grow and adapt to our environments, which inevitably affects the way we look at life. Associations and experiences play a significant role, and the home environment—our parents coupled with what we've heard, seen or felt—is a very effective sculpting tool.

The nature of many individuals is to look for what's wrong or the negative in everything. It may even be an occupational habit for some people. Still, many others are able to maintain a positive outlook, even in challenging situations.

For the optimist, everything is great; their glass is half full. For the pessimist, something could always be better. Truthfully, there's a positive and negative side within all of us, but one side seems to be more dominant.

There is a dominant element that optimistic people possess. The element is hope. The Bible says in Hebrews 6:19 (NIV), "We have this hope as an anchor for the soul, firm and secure…." In this verse, the Apostle Paul, the writer of Hebrews, identified hope as an anchor for the soul (the emotions).

Without hope, you have nothing to anchor your emotions to keep them from drifting. You simply flow like an ocean current. Without an anchor to steady your feelings, you find yourself in despair, wandering aimlessly.

The Apostle Paul wrote in 1 Thessalonians 5:8 (NIV), "But since we belong to the day, let us be sober, putting on faith and love as a breastplate, and the hope of salvation as a helmet." That is an interesting perspective—we should wear "hope" as a helmet. The helmet of hope is to be worn to secure our soul (emotions). Consequently, if we fail to accept hope, then destructive, negative emotions like discouragement, depression, loneliness, and bitterness can take us out.

The beauty of hope is that it gives us the determination to achieve God's plan for our lives in spite of circumstances. Below are a few attributes of hope.

- Hope is the confident expectation of a better future.

- Hope hangs onto the promise, overcomes adversity, pursues truth, and endures patiently.

- Hope holds on; pain ends.

- Hope hangs onto positive energy.

- Hope holds on while patiently expecting.

- Hope is sure of what it does not see, persevering to procure, eagerly doing and enduring.

THE ROAD TO NOWHERE

Has anyone ever told you that you have a bad attitude? Has anyone ever said to you, "Looks like you woke up on the wrong side of the bed"? That's negativity.

Negativity is described as an attitude that only sees the wrong, is highly critical, and complaining. A negative person is someone who is unpleasant, gloomy, unfavorable, and resistant. They are the ones who think, *It's never going to happen, It'll always be this way, or It's never going to work.*

Remember the story of Winnie the Pooh? One of his friends is a donkey called Eeyore. Eeyore lives in a beautiful forest, has amazing friends, but is always negative about life.

To display negative emotions is normal; everyone does from time to time. To exhibit negative emotions consistently, or more often than not, is abnormal and can be toxic.

For years, psychologists have studied the connection between positive emotions and negative emotions and how they impact our immune system. Dr. Tony Jimenez, the Medical Director of Hope for Cancer Institute, said, "Negative thoughts kill a person faster than bad germs."

The study and research on positive emotions versus negative emotions continues and is gaining ground as it includes many well-respected doctors in the field of medicine and psychology. Several have gathered data and developed something called an Emotional Pain Chart, which shows how your body reacts to negative emotions.

You and I experience all kinds of emotions every day—from happiness to sadness and, at times, even depression. Emotions affect the body, which is evident in how the body responds to the way we think and feel. The Emotional Pain Chart, a diagram of the body, pinpoints the connection between the body and emotions and reveals why emotional pain becomes physical pain.

Did you know that your body has an active frequency or electrical energy? It can be detected with the aid of a highly sensitive device. Well, negative emotions throw your frequency off; it becomes imbalanced. To have a healthy body is to have healthy energy or a healthy frequency, but when you display negative emotions, the frequency is counterproductive. It would be as disturbing internally as the sound of nails being dragged across a chalkboard.

I don't know about you, but I don't want to have any negative frequency coming out of me. The thought of nails on a chalkboard is enough to want to change.

When you walk in unforgiveness, bitterness, jealousy, or other negative emotions, you can impact your kidneys, heart, liver, colon, and other organs. You may be able to withstand the effects for a while before symptoms arise, but the longer you hold onto those feelings, the greater the impact. The negativity that's being sustained may give way to intestinal or hormonal problems as the body tries to figure out how to counterattack the prevailing effects of negative emotions. Unfortunately, as time goes on, the internal changes may become increasingly harmful. On the outside, you're still the cute version of yourself. You style and profile. You have your nails and your hair done, and everything looks just right. On the inside, you're different. The effects of holding onto the emotional pain are severely affecting you.

We can't allow negative emotions to remain and believe they won't cause damage. You wouldn't allow a rodent in your house and assume that it won't cause damage, would you? So, what is the solution?

The Bible provides answers for those seeking to overcome negative emotions. Let's take a look at the following scriptures:

"Casting all your care upon Him, for He cares for you."
—1 Peter 5:7

"Resist the devil and he will flee from you."
—James 4:7

"'Is not My word like a fire?' says the Lord, 'And like a hammer that breaks the rock in pieces?'"
—Jeremiah 23:29

"But thou art holy, O thou that inhabitest the praises of Israel."
—Psalm 22:3 (KJV)

"You have established a stronghold against your enemies, to silence the foe and the avenger."
—Psalm 8:2 (NIV)

"Be careful for nothing; but in everything by prayer and supplication with thanksgiving, let your requests be made known unto God. And the peace of God, which passeth all understanding, shall keep your hearts and minds through Christ Jesus."
—Philippians 4:6-7 (KJV)

Perhaps you've read some or all of the verses before, but have you ever put them into practice? Consider what 2 Timothy 3:16 (NLT) tells us:

All Scripture is inspired by God and is useful to teach us what is true and to make us realize what is wrong in our lives. It corrects us when we are wrong and teaches us to do what is right.

Let me emphasize the words "teaches us to do." The Word is not just to be read but to be carried out as instructed. According to the scriptures above, we are to cast, resist, praise, and pray, which will help us overcome negative emotions.

The Bible also tells us to meditate on the Word. The word "meditation" has been associated with Eastern gurus or new age philosophy and, on occasion, has been deemed cultish. Yet, the Bible repeatedly encourages us to meditate on God's Word. God wants us to meditate (to focus our thoughts) on Him over our daily routines, which feeds our faith.

Meditation is like a sprinkler system that waters the seeds of faith you've planted. Planting the seed isn't enough, but watering it every day will cause it to root, grow, and bear fruit. Read the Word, say it out loud, and think about it. Doing this over and over is the key.

It's said we are to chew our food 32 times before swallowing. Treat mediation like that—chew, chew, and chew some more.

The following scriptures are just a few that reference meditation:

"Keep this Book of the Law always on your lips; meditate on it day and night, so that you may be careful to do everything written in it. Then you will be prosperous and successful."

—Joshua 1:8 (NIV)

"But his delight is in the law of the LORD, And in His law he meditates day and night."

—Psalm 1:2

"Let the words of my mouth and the meditation of my heart be acceptable in Your sight, O LORD, my strength and my Redeemer."

—Psalm 19:14

"May all my thoughts be pleasing to Him, for I rejoice in the LORD."

—Psalm 104:34 (NLT)

As Christians, we are to take some time out from our busy lives to be still and meditate daily on at least one or two Bible verses. That is especially so when we are dealing with overwhelming circumstances. As you commit to this daily discipline, your mind will be renewed.

SEEING THE BIG PICTURE

Visualization can be used to detoxify your mind and change the way you think. God used visualization with Abram.

We read the following in Genesis 13:14-17:

And the LORD said to Abram, after Lot had separated from him: 'Lift your eyes now and look from the place where you are—northward, southward, eastward, and westward; for all the land which you see I give to you and your descendants forever. And I will make your descendants as the dust of the earth; so that if a man could number the dust of the earth, then your descendants also could be numbered. Arise, walk in the land through its length and its width, for I give it to you.'

God spoke life to Abram by encouraging him to visualize his future.

You may have been devalued or rejected at some time in your life. Perhaps it happened during your childhood, in your marriage, or on your job. It's time for you to start believing in your future by detoxifying your mind of the past.

Meditating on what God says about you and what He has for you, before the promise manifests, is an act of faith. Seeing your marriage restored while you're still fussing and fighting, seeing your body healed while it's wracked with disease, or seeing yourself free from debt while overwhelmed by it is about visualizing your circumstances the way God sees them. Visualization requires action on your part, and you have to commit to it for change to occur in your life.

Maintaining good physical health is also essential. There are many people who are beautifully saved and prosperous in earthly goods but have neglected the temple (the body). What do I mean by that? In 3 John 1:2, we read, "Beloved, I pray that you may prosper in all things and be in health, just as your soul prospers." According to this verse, not only are we supposed to prosper in natural and spiritual things, but we should also have high standards for our bodies. When the body is wracked with disease, it affects one's thinking, and negative emotions further diminish one's health.

When I used to run marathons, I was in good shape. I had five percent body fat. I, in fact, qualified for the Boston Marathon, which is the most elite marathon in the nation. To run in that marathon, you must qualify; you can't just sign up. I'm not bragging but describing the caliber of runner I was to better illustrate the point.

People would come up to me and say, "Man, you're healthy!" What they didn't know was that cancer was growing in my body, even though I had not been diagnosed with the illness, nor was I taking medication. Although I appeared to be in good shape, qualified for and ran the Boston Marathon, my outward appearance wasn't an accurate depiction of my overall health.

Realize that you can look good on the outside, but do you know what's really going on inside of you? You may appear to be in shape but are you healthy?

God is concerned about everything about you. It is God's will that you prosper in every area of your life. He is concerned about your physical body prospering, and He is concerned about you prospering spiritually. He is concerned about you prospering financially, and He is also concerned about your soul (your mind and emotions) prospering. He doesn't want us to neglect our bodies. You and I are triune beings—spirit, soul, and body—and each area affects the other.

The Apostle Paul, in his letter to the church at Thessalonica, talked about the whole man when he said, "May your whole spirit, soul and body be preserved blameless at the coming of our Lord Jesus Christ" (1 Thessalonians 5:23). God wants us to fulfill the call He has placed on our lives, to die old and full of days as Job did.

To be in good health is not automatic. Something is required of us if we want it. Hippocrates said, "If someone wishes for good health, one must first ask oneself if he is ready to do away with the reason for the illness. Only then is it possible to help him." There is a cost associated with being a healthy, whole, and sound person. Not everyone is willing to pay the price.

BEING OF SOUND MIND

When people hear the name "Jabez," most think of a well-respected man in the Old Testament whose prayer was answered when he prayed for God's blessing (1 Chronicles 4:9-10). Most people don't know that prior to God answering Jabez's prayer, he was surrounded by negativity. His mother named him Jabez, which means pain and sorrow. Perhaps the reason for his name was because his mother's labor was very long and excruciating.

The name Jabez embodies negativity, so wherever he went in life, that negativity accompanied him. Whether he was at school, with his family, friends, or elsewhere, every time he heard his name, it was like hearing, "Hey, Pain, come here." "How are you, Pain?" How would you like to be labeled as pain?

One day Jabez rejected the negativity associated with his name by rising up and crying out boldly to the God of Israel. 1 Chronicles 4:10 states, "Oh, that you would bless me and enlarge my territory! Let your hand be with me, and keep me from harm so that I will be free from pain." God granted Jabez's request.

The amazing truth is that regardless of our past, once we decide to reject the negativity in our lives and develop a close relationship with God, our whole lives change. Jabez was honored by God when he cried out. God heard his prayer and blessed him.

There are a number of individuals found in the Bible, like Jabez, who took a stand in the midst of adverse circumstances. For instance, Joseph was surrounded by his brothers' negativity. They did not believe that he would ever be a leader or that God would ever use him.

Ruth had to overcome the negativity she experienced as a result of losing her husband and the uncertainty of her future. There was no welfare program to depend on, and going to a foreign country most likely added to her already stressful circumstance.

Jephthah, in the book of Judges, was called a mighty man of valor. In other words, he was a mighty warrior. However, he had to overcome negativity in his life because his mother was a prostitute. When people looked at him, they didn't necessarily see his potential or his desire to do something for God. What most saw was the child of a prostitute, but he became a great judge despite his lineage.

The greatest example we can learn from when it comes to

overcoming negativity is Jesus. He was victorious in the face of persecution, temptation, and torture. He faced disapproval from the religious and political leaders of His day. His family and friends didn't believe in Him. Jesus faced the antagonism of the devil who harassed and tempted Him. Yet, the Bible tells us in Acts 10:38, "How God anointed Jesus of Nazareth with the Holy Spirit and with power, who went about doing good...." He never let the negativity stop Him from doing good and accomplishing what God called Him to do.

A MATTER OF PERSPECTIVE

In Numbers 13 and 14, the story of the children of Israel unfolds as they journey through the wilderness. God promised to give Abraham a land called Canaan. It was described as a rich, flourishing land, which basically meant that everything he could imagine was there.

Fast-forward approximately 400 years; the children of Israel were finally free from Egyptian bondage. If you have ever watched the movie *The Ten Commandments,* you saw the depiction of their dramatic departure from Egypt. When they arrived at the Red Sea, it divided in front of their eyes so that they could cross over and make their way to Canaan.

During their journey to Canaan, Moses chose one leader from each of the twelve tribes to go and spy out the land. He wanted them to go ahead and bring back a report about the people and land they were to encounter before the multitude moved forward. After 40 days of spying out the land, the twelve leaders returned.

They brought back grapes, pomegranates, and figs from the land that they explored. In Numbers 13:23 (NIV), it says, "They cut off a branch bearing a single cluster of grapes. Two of them carried it on a pole between them, along with some pomegranates and figs."

Think about that; they had never seen fruit like that before. We can only imagine the commotion among the children of Israel when the leaders returned with all that incredible produce. I'm sure in those days, they didn't realize that the nutritional gems they found were filled with life-giving antioxidants to keep their bodies healthy.

When the children of Israel saw the fruit, it was confirmation of what God had promised them. Unfortunately, ten leaders brought back a negative report; only two gave a positive report—Joshua and Caleb. In Numbers 13:27-33 (NIV), we read the following:

> They gave Moses this account: 'We went into the land to which you sent us, and it does flow with milk and honey! Here is its fruit. But the people who live there are powerful, and the cities are fortified and very large. We even saw descendants of Anak [giants] there. The Amalekites live in the Negev; the Hittites, Jebusites and Amorites live in the hill country; and the Canaanites live near the sea and along the Jordan.'
>
> Then Caleb silenced the people before Moses and said, 'We should go up and take possession of the land, for we can certainly do it.'
>
> The men who had gone up with him said, 'We can't

attack those people; they are stronger than we are....
The land we explored devours those living in it. All the
people we saw there are of great size.... We seemed like
grasshoppers in our own eyes, and we looked the same
to them.'

Negative people look at the obstacles and want to give up. The
leaders who went with Caleb and Joshua filled the people with
fear and confusion. It takes strong leaders like Caleb and Joshua
to encourage, uplift, and keep people focused, especially among
negative leaders like the other ten spies.

Strong leaders never look at their circumstances as impossible.
They see the possibility in everything. When others see
blockades, great leaders see challenges to overcome. They find
ways to let go of the negativity that holds others back. Dwight
D. Eisenhower said, "Always try to associate yourself with and
learn as much as you can from those who know more than you
do, who do better than you, who see more clearly than you."

What lessons can we learn from the story of the twelve spies?
Well, let's begin with the ten negative spies. They saw the
inhabitants of the land as too big to conquer. It's important
to note that whenever you decide to take action to possess a
promise, there will be giants or obstacles in your way, but they
aren't always harmful or bad.

I believe the giants we face are signposts indicating that we're
headed in the right direction. Victories don't come without
opposition. Since God doesn't give us a complete road map
or agenda for life's journeys, we must consider that whatever

God is doing will involve some meddling or interference from the enemy before the promised victory. Remember, before the people of Israel faced the obstacles and negative report given by the spies, God promised to give them the land. Caleb and Joshua kept their focus on the promised blessing while the ten spies were focused on the alleged dangers.

Negative people have a tendency to exaggerate and distort circumstances. In the case of the men who went with Caleb and Joshua, they said, "The land we explored *devours* those living in it. *All* the people we saw there are of great size. We saw the Nephilim there [descendants of Anak come from the Nephilim]. *We seemed* like grasshoppers...."

You may know people who exaggerate and lean towards negative statements. They make comments like, "I've been miserable *all* my life," "You have *never* done me right," "You *never* listen to me," or "*All* people are the same."

The negativity spewed by the ten spies impacted the outlook of others. Look at what the Bible says in Numbers 14:2-4:

> All the Israelites grumbled against Moses and Aaron, and the whole assembly said to them, 'If only we had died in Egypt! Or in this wilderness! Why is the LORD bringing us to this land only to let us fall by the sword? Our wives and children will be taken as plunder. Wouldn't it be better for us to go back to Egypt?' And they said to each other, 'We should choose a leader and go back to Egypt.'

Excuse me, but did the children of Israel forget what life was like back in Egypt?

155

After 430 years of slavery, taskmasters, Pharaoh, and much more, God delivered them from the heavy hand of Pharaoh. Because of the perceived adversity experienced by ten of the twelve spies, the nation wanted to return to a state of bondage, struggle, and lack. They were willing to be at the mercy of a person and a system that formed a victim mentality.

We're not to dwell on the past. That doesn't get us anywhere. In Isaiah 43:18-19 (NIV), we read:

> Forget the former things; do not dwell on the past. See, I am doing a new thing! Now it springs up; do you not perceive it? I am making a way in the wilderness and streams in the wasteland.

I can hear the violin being played in the background as the people complain to each other about their desire to go back to Egypt. The negative spirit had infiltrated the Israelite camp, and it spread like wildfire.

Negativity is a stronghold on a person's mind. It's only through the power of the Holy Spirit that the negative stronghold can be broken; only then can a person experience true freedom.

I encourage you to read the entire story in Numbers 13 and 14, and learn what happened to the ten spies and the people. Many died with their negativity and never possessed the blessings of God. They never walked in what God had for them because of the complaining and unbelief. Though they saw and tasted the grapes, though they saw and tasted the pomegranates and figs, it was only for a moment when it could have been for a lifetime.

THE POWER OF WORDS

Do you know that words are powerful and capable of generating life? Once words leave your mouth, they have the power to evoke love or hate; to be positive or negative. It all depends on how influential the source is and the vulnerability of the receiver.

Generally, what we say gives people a glimpse of who we are. We have to watch the words that we allow to come out of our mouths. Why? Because Proverbs 18:21 (NIV) says, "The tongue has the power of life and death, and those who love it will eat its fruit." That is not some psychosomatic belief; that is the gospel.

God spoke the worlds into existence. Psalm 33:6 (NIV) states, "By the word of the LORD the heavens were made, their starry host by the breath of His mouth." In Psalm 33:9 (NIV), we read, "For He spoke, and it came to be; He commanded, and it stood firm."

Jesus used words to curse the fig tree, and it dried up (Mark 11:14). In Mark 11:23, Jesus said, "Whoever says to this mountain, 'Be removed and be cast into the sea,' and does not doubt in his heart, but believes that those things he says will be done, he will have whatever he says." These verses are amazing!

Imagine your words having the power to bring life or death to every area of your life. Your children are blessed based upon your words. Your future is blessed based upon your words. Your health is blessed based upon your words. Your finances and your destiny are blessed based upon your words.

On the other hand, if the words you speak sound something like,

"I'll never…," "I'm a failure," "It's impossible," "It ain't gonna happen," or "It's too hard," then know that you're speaking that into your future. Mother Teresa said, "Words which do not give the light of Christ increase the darkness."

When I was a little boy, my mom would take me into the bathroom, and I'd literally have my mouth washed out with soap if I said a curse word. I don't know if you had a mom like mine, but my mom would do that to teach me that she didn't want anything dirty to come out of my mouth. Could that also be God's desire?

We're going to mess up every once in a while, but God wants His Word to wash out all that negativity. He wants us to get into His Word and say what His Word says about our situations.

Stop saying what you feel. Stop saying what someone else said about you. Stop saying what you're experiencing. Stop saying what you heard and say only what He says about you and your situation.

David wrote in Psalm 19:14, "Let the words of my mouth and the meditation of my heart be acceptable in Your sight, O LORD, my strength and my Redeemer."

Keep in mind that it's very important that you know enough of the Bible to know what God says about your circumstances so that the words coming out of your mouth line up with His Word.

It's interesting to note that when you or I go to see a doctor, one of the ways the doctor attempts to determine what's wrong is to ask you to open your mouth, stick out your tongue, and say, "Ahhh." Evidently, there's a possibility that your mouth will reveal the problem. In the same way, when you're having problems in your life, your mouth will reveal the problems or your mouth will speak His words of life.

Another thing that I recognize in the story about the twelve spies is that the men who went with Caleb and Joshua focused on the giants. They said, "There we saw giants...and we were like grasshoppers in our own sight."

Think about that for a minute. Instead of seeing themselves as able-bodied men, they saw themselves as unworthy, no-good losers and defeated failures before the fight ever began. They did not see themselves as giant killers. They did not see themselves as people who could overcome opposition. They saw themselves as grasshoppers—little bitty, unworthy nobodies. Because they thought that, they spoke and projected that.

The Bible tells us in Proverbs 23:7 (KJV), "For as he thinketh in his heart, so is he...." You better pay attention to what you think about and the images you allow to overtake your mind because what you consistently think, you will likely manifest.

Have you ever thought, *I don't know why this happens all the time, or I don't know why I always attract that type of person*? It happens because you first thought it.

Have you ever noticed someone who's attractive and smart, and then you noticed the person they were dating? Some may have seemed to be an unlikely pair. When you really understand what Proverbs 23:7 means, you can better understand why they're together. Many people believe they will never find someone who truly loves and appreciates them for who they are, so they willingly settle for less. They lower their standards to fit the image they perceive of themselves.

RIGHT THINKING

If you're like me, you always have your mobile phone with you, and it's not uncommon to glance at your phone and notice that you have thirty new emails, and most of them are junk mail.

I am obsessive! As soon as I see email notifications, I have to clear them. Soon after, though, I receive another series of emails. It drives me crazy! If I put off looking at my phone for about an hour, boom! Twenty or thirty more emails show up, and I do the same thing all over again.

My wife couldn't care less about her emails. If you saw her phone, it would probably indicate that she has 5,299 messages. No matter how many emails are waiting to be opened, Cindy is in no rush to open them; she doesn't worry about them.

When the enemy sends you an email (figuratively) that says, *You're a loser, you're hopeless, you're not going to amount to anything*, don't sit there and dwell on the message, and don't allow it to distract you from the promises of God. When negative messages bombard your mind, delete them just as you do on your devices. If you don't, then the negative messages may produce a grasshopper mentality. That may keep you from entering into God's best for you, as was the situation involving the ten spies.

In Philippians 4:8 (NIV), the Bible tells us, "Finally, brothers and sisters, whatever is true, whatever is noble, whatever is right, whatever is pure, whatever is lovely, whatever is admirable—if anything is excellent or praiseworthy—think about such things." This verse clearly tells us what we should be thinking about. Why then do we waste time thinking about the bad things that happened to us or what someone did to us? Why do we dwell on why we were denied or rejected? Why think about the shame, guilt, and condemnation? We need to focus our thoughts on what is pure and lovely, not the unfavorable events.

When I was diagnosed with cancer in 2008, I was very mindful of the words I spoke. If you hung around me and didn't know my condition, you wouldn't have known that I had cancer because I didn't talk like a cancer victim. I monitored my words because I knew life and death were in the power of my tongue.

People who were aware of my condition would approach me and ask, "Diego, how are you feeling?" They didn't hear me say, *I feel lousy,* or *I'm tore up about this disease.* Instead, I would answer with something like, "It doesn't matter how I'm feeling. By faith, in the name of Jesus, I'm healed."

Let me tell you how methodical I was about what I said. I did not call it cancer; I renamed it. I called it an attack because I did not want to give life to cancer and make it bigger than it was. I watched what I said about other things too. I didn't use terms like *my doctor, my appointment, my medication.* They were not mine. It was nailed to the cross. I didn't want to confess ownership of it.

During that time, I monitored my thoughts and was careful about what I listened to because I knew that what I meditated on could manifest.

I learned how to visualize, which helped me tremendously. I'd go and look at the mountains that I used to run on in Rancho Cucamonga at Lytle Creek. I'd look at them, and I'd talk to them. I'd say, "I'm going to run you again," and I would visualize myself running up the mountain.

One day, I bought new running shoes, even though I wasn't going to wear them anytime soon. I remember looking at those shoes and saying, "I'm going to wear you one day, but for now, I'm going to put you in the box." Another day I took the shoes out of the box and put them on just to feel them on my feet. I knew there would come a day when I would put them on to run the mountains again, and I did.

You may be thinking, *That's stupid; I don't believe in that.* Unless you've been diagnosed with stage 4 cancer, you probably wouldn't understand. For me, I needed to visualize what I believed.

I also visualized myself riding my bike again.

One day, my wife Cindy saw me headed in the direction of the garage, and she asked me, "What are you going to do there?"

I told Cindy, "I'm going to clean off my road bike."

Cindy replied, "You know you can't ride it."

"I know," I said, "but I'm going to clean it because one day I am going to ride it."

I spent thirty minutes out there. The tires were flat, so I pumped them up. I even oiled the chain. The next thing I knew, I was going inside the house to put on all my biking gear.

My wife said, "What are you doing? You can't bike."

"Well, I don't know…take a picture of me." I sat on the bike to pose for the shot.

I didn't ride that day, but the day came when I would, and I haven't stopped since.

You don't have to be diagnosed with a disease to visualize. When you visualize, you are characterizing faith in action, which you can use in any area of your life.

Remember, God used visualization when He told Abram to look up to the sky and count the stars, and the promise was granted to Abram because of his faith. The Bible tells us in Romans 4:17-18:

> As it is written, 'I have made you a father of many nations in the presence of Him whom he believed—God, who gives life to the dead and calls those things which do not exist as though they did; who, contrary to hope, in hope believed, so that he became the father of many nations, according to what was spoken, 'So shall your descendants be.'

We see a similar description of faith in 2 Corinthians 4:18, which states, "While we do not look at the things which are seen, but at the things which are not seen. For the things which are seen are temporary, but the things which are not seen are eternal."

If you're single and asking God to bring you a mate, place a wedding picture on your table at home. Purchase a wedding album. Get a wedding brochure to review as if you're making plans for your special day. Separate yourself from negativity and visualize your future. That's what Caleb and Joshua did; they separated themselves from the ten spies and saw God's promise.

Know that you cannot hang around negative people and hope that their negativity won't rub off on you. Remember, the Bible says, "Caleb quieted the people," and sometimes you've got to tell the person bringing negativity into your life to be quiet. At times, you may just have to walk away and ignore them. Whatever you do, don't tolerate their negativity.

As I stated, be mindful of what you listen to, including the music that entertains you. Don't say to yourself, "It's just music," because it's more than that. It produces images and has the potential to influence behavior.

The same is true about what you watch on television. A thirty-minute television program, a two-hour movie, and a three-minute song can influence you in ways you never considered.

When I was young, there was a television cartoon called Gulliver's Travels, and there was a character named Glomb. Glomb's favorite line was, "It will never work." Gulliver desired to travel, explore, and pioneer new adventures, but Glomb's opinion was, "It will never work." Has there ever been a Glomb in your life telling you that whatever you want to do will never work or never happen for you?

When Caleb and Joshua faced the crowd that received the negative report from the ten spies, the Bible tells us in Numbers 14:6-9 that Caleb and Joshua tore their clothes and spoke the following to the children of Israel:

> The land we passed through to spy out is an exceedingly good land. If the Lord delights in us, then He will bring us into this land and give it to us, a land which flows with milk and honey. Only do not *rebel* against the Lord, nor fear the people of the land, for they are our bread; their protection has departed from them, and the Lord is with us. Do not fear them.

Negativity is a form of rebellion wherein a person doubts God's ability to rescue, heal, restore, or produce. It's questioning whether God *can* change a negative circumstance to a positive outcome.

The children of Israel rose in rebellion against God after they heard the negative report. Their disbelief said, "God can't overcome the giants. God can't give us the land. We will never be what God wants us to be."

God took their rebellion personal. Numbers 14:26-27 reads, "And the Lord spoke to Moses and Aaron, saying, 'How long shall I bear with this evil congregation who complain against Me? I have heard the complaints which the children of Israel make against Me.'"

In essence, their doubt questioned who He was and magnified their fears.

The truth of God's sovereignty is that although they rebelled, God would eventually fulfill His promise. Unfortunately, a generation would die off before it was fulfilled.

FAITH TO OVERCOME

One of my life's verses is found in words Caleb spoke: "Let us go up at once and take possession, for we are well able to overcome it" (Numbers 13:30). I speak this verse over absolutely anything and everything that comes my way.

Other scriptures that I quote in challenging situations include the following:

> "All things work together for good to those who love God."
> —Romans 8:28

> "You meant evil against me; but God meant it for good...."
> —Genesis 50:20

And one of my favorite positive, optimistic, hope-filled, faith-filled verses...

> "We are hard-pressed on every side, yet not crushed. We are perplexed, but not in despair; persecuted, but not forsaken; struck down, but not destroyed."
> —2 Corinthians 4:8-9

I believe it's important to have purposeful moments of meditation (thinking) every day because it helps to keep negativity away. For me, it goes something like this:

- First, I think about what I am grateful for, and I express gratitude to God for those things.

- Second, I think about something I still have to accomplish, something positive I'm looking forward to.

- Third, I think about one person who is important to me, someone I need to live for.

- Finally, I ask myself how I can change or who I can help.

When you feel depressed, when you feel defeated, when you feel paralyzed and unable to move forward, let these four thoughts rise up in you. Allow them to give you purpose to go on because there's still someone you have to help; there are still things you have to accomplish.

In closing, I'll share a funny story with you.

A lady went to see her hairdresser in preparation for a dream vacation with her husband. As the hairdresser began to style her hair, she asked the woman where she was going.

"I'm going to Rome," the woman answered.

The hairdresser responded, "Rome? Who wants to go to Rome? Everything costs too much over there; the euro is, you know, going up. It's dirty, and it's overcrowded. You're crazy to want to go to Rome. How are you going to get there?"

The woman answered, "We're flying…" and she identified the airlines.

The hairdresser replied, "That airline's rates are astronomical, the planes are old, and the flight attendants are nasty." After a brief pause, the hairdresser asked, "Where are you going to stay in Rome?"

"Well," the woman answered hesitantly, "I'm going to stay at the Ra…"

Before she could even finish her sentence, the hairdresser interrupted and said, "That hotel? It is a rat-hole! Their service stinks. I'm very familiar with that place. It's a dump!" Next, the hairdresser asked, "What are you going to do in Rome?"

The woman responded cautiously, "I'm going to go to the Vatican."

Speaking in the same tone of voice, the hairdresser responded, "The Vatican? You want to see the Pope? You know that about a billion people want to see the Pope, and you think you're going to get close to him? That's going to be one of the lousiest trips that you'll ever take."

A month later, the lady returned to the salon to have her hair done. As soon as the woman was seated, her hairdresser asked, "Hey, how was that trip to Rome?"

The woman replied, "It was wonderful! It was the best vacation I've ever taken in my life! The city was beautiful. The airlines recently put a new fleet of airplanes in service, and the flight attendants were very nice. The hotel we stayed in recently spent $50,000,000 on renovations. It was heavily booked, but they upgraded us to a suite and took good care of us. We did everything we wanted to do while we were in Rome."

Surprised by the woman's report of the trip, the hairdresser asked, "Well, what about going to see the Pope at the Vatican; did you do that?"

The woman answered, "Well, you'll never guess what happened. I was there, and all of a sudden, the Swiss Guard approached me and said, 'Rarely does this happen, but every once in a while, the Pope may ask us to pull people out for a brief but personal conversation with him,' and to my surprise, I was chosen."

"Oh, really?" her hairdresser responded. "What did he say to you?"

"He asked me, 'Who in the heck did your hair?'"

The moral of the story is that there are many negative Nancys in this world, and I'm sure you have met your fair share of them. Don't let them rain on your parade or stop you from enjoying life to the fullest. God has promised you a better future. Remember, He is always with you, so trust Him for all your tomorrows.

Prayer

Father, I thank you that you give me hope for my life today. I ask you to deliver me from my negative attitude. Help me to see things in my life as half full and not half empty.

I put on the helmet of hope to protect me, and I anchor my soul in hope to bless me. My hope is in you, Lord, and I believe the best is yet to come. No matter what life looks like right now, I know that it's temporary and subject to change because you, Lord, are my hope now and eternally.

In Jesus' name. Amen.

Questions

When you look at your life in general, do you see it as half full or half empty? Explain your answer.

_____

_____

_____

_____

Do you notice a difference in your overall health when you speak or act negatively instead of positively? Give an example.

_____

_____

_____

Proverbs 18:21 (NIV) says, "The tongue has the power of life and death, and those who love it will eat its fruit." In your own words, explain this scripture.

_____

_____

_____

_____

Proverbs 23:7 tells us, "For as he thinks in his heart, so is he...." How important is it for us to be careful of our thought-life? Give an example of when you chose between right and wrong thinking.

_____

_____

_____

_____

Additional Notes:

_____

_____

_____

_____

CHAPTER 6

NO MORE SORROW, NO MORE TEARS

In all these things we are more than conquerors through Him who loved us. For I am sure that neither death nor life, nor angels nor rulers, nor things present nor things to come, nor powers, nor height nor depth, nor anything else in all creation, will be able to separate us from the love of God in Christ Jesus our Lord.
—Romans 8:37-39 (NIV)

When you hear the phrase "No More Tears," do you connect it with a slogan for baby shampoo? If so, you're not alone. In 1953, Johnson & Johnson Baby Shampoo's debut was promoted as a very mild shampoo perfect for a baby's sensitive skin. The "No More Tears" promotion suggested that even if some shampoo got into a child's eyes during bath time, it was so gentle it wouldn't burn.

The product won the hearts of millions, eliminating the daily drama experienced during bath time for babies and parents.

In 2005, a documentary was produced to chronicle the lives of eight children who survived the December 2004 Indian Ocean earthquake and tsunami (also known as the Boxing Day Tsunami) that occurred off the west coast of northern Sumatra, Indonesia. The earthquake registered a magnitude of 9.1 to 9.3 and produced a series of tsunami waves up to 100 feet high. As a result, an estimated 227,898 people in 14 countries lost their lives.

The documentary was titled *Children of Tsunami: No More Tears*. It depicts the aftermath and horrific suffering, sorrow, and grief experienced by the children and their families who lost loved ones, homes, personal possessions, and their livelihood. It details the challenges they faced during their journey to rebuild their shattered lives. The amazing story is a true testament to the human spirit's determined will to live on after tragedy.

Whether tears are shed by an innocent child during bath time or children who experienced tragic loss, the ultimate desire of those close to them is to undo the hurt and restore their emotional state back to normal. Well, who can best understand the depth of our souls and the anguish we suffer during emotional distress but the Creator? He designed us with the ability to release tears of sadness. Additionally, according to 1 Peter 5:7, we're encouraged to cast our cares upon Him.

There comes the point in life when we must say, "I'm not crying about that anymore. I've been crying over that too long." To do that, we must put our pain and sorrow in proper perspective so that we can move on.

When I think about having no more sorrow and no more tears,

I'm reminded of the story of Joshua, who led the people of Israel after Moses' death. The Bible states the following in Joshua 1:1-2:

> After the death of Moses, the servant of the Lord, it came to pass that the Lord spoke to Joshua the son of Nun, Moses' assistant, saying: 'Moses My servant is dead. Now therefore, arise, go over this Jordan, you and all this people, to the land which I am giving to them—the children of Israel.'

Joshua could have chosen to mourn Moses' death for a long time, but he chose to follow the leading of the Lord. According to verse 11, Joshua issued a command to the officers of the people.

> Pass through the camp and command the people, saying, 'Prepare provisions for yourself, for within three days you will cross over this Jordan, to go in to possess the land which the LORD your God is giving you to possess.

So often we mourn for people, things, and situations longer than we should, and that can become very unhealthy. It can actually stop us from moving forward. When that happens, we don't fulfill the destiny that God has for us.

Moses and Joshua spent forty years together. They were lifelong friends. I'm sure that Joshua grieved when Moses died, but when God spoke to him, he knew it was time to move forward and lead the people as Moses led them. If Joshua had stopped, he would not have inherited the Promised Land, and he and the children of Israel would not have fulfilled the destiny that God had for them.

There is a time to grieve a loss, and for everyone, it's different, just as reactions, expressions, and feelings differ. It's completely acceptable. However, we can't remain in a state of sorrow.

HEALING THE BROKENHEARTED

The Bible reveals that Jesus knew how it felt to be human. He was sympathetic and understood human weaknesses and temptations. We read the following in Hebrews 4:15-16 (AMP):

> For we do not have a High Priest who is unable to sympathize and understand our weaknesses and temptations, but One who has been tempted [knowing exactly how it feels to be human] in every respect as we are, yet without [committing any] sin.

> Therefore let us [with privilege] approach the throne of grace [that is, the throne of God's gracious favor] with confidence and without fear, so that we may receive mercy [for our failures] and find [His amazing] grace to help in time of need [an appropriate blessing, coming just at the right moment].

Jesus experienced grief when John the Baptist, His relative, was executed. They were only six months apart in age, and no doubt the families were close and experienced life together.

The Bible records in Matthew 14:3-10 that John was imprisoned and beheaded by Herod the tetrarch because John rebuked him of his marriage to Herodias, his brother's wife.

After burying his body, John's disciples went and told Jesus what occurred (verse 12). The Bible tells us that when Jesus heard the news, He left in a boat to a remote area to be alone (verse 13). Jesus wanted some alone time.

In verses 13-14 (NLT) we read, "But the crowds heard where He was headed and followed on foot from many towns. Jesus saw the huge crowd as He stepped from the boat, and He had compassion on them and healed their sick."

Even though Jesus wanted to be alone, the compassion He felt for the people was greater than His desire. What Jesus felt for the crowd of people compelled Him to continue to act according to His purpose as stated in Isaiah 61:1 and Luke 4:18.

The Spirit of the Lord is upon Me, because the Lord has anointed Me to preach good tidings to the poor; He has sent Me to heal the brokenhearted, to proclaim liberty to the captives, and the opening of the prison to those who are bound.

You may say, "But that's Jesus." Yes, that's true. Remember, though, what's stated in Hebrews 4:15 (AMP), "One who has been tempted [knowing exactly how it feels to be human] in every respect as we are...." Jesus felt grief for John, but He knew the crowd needed a healer to heal their brokenness.

PROCESSING GRIEF AND SORROW

To grieve and be sorrowful when we experience loss is expected. It's important to know that there is a good process for grief. What do I mean by that? Good sadness or good grief is when a person can recover emotionally within a healthy period as opposed to finding it difficult to recover from a loss.

Wikipedia has an interesting article on a condition known as Complicated Grief Disorder. It states the following:

> In psychiatry, complicated grief disorder (CGD) is a proposed disorder for those who are significantly and functionally impaired by prolonged grief symptoms for at least one month after six months of bereavement. Complicated grief is considered when an individual's ability to resume normal activities and responsibilities is continually disrupted beyond six months of bereavement. Six months is considered to be the appropriate point of CGD consideration, since studies show that most people are able to integrate bereavement into their lives by this time.

When someone experiences loss, a series of reactions naturally occur as the individual processes the loss. The initial reactions are shock and denial. Most cannot believe what has happened. They go numb to the situation and don't know how to move past it. They tell themselves, "This isn't happening; this can't be real."

Once reality sets in, individuals may feel like they're on an emotional roller coaster. They're not sure how to react. They feel angry, guilty, depressed, and lonely. There's no right or wrong order for these emotions.

The final phases are acceptance and recovery, and here is where a lot of people fall short. It's understood that grief is difficult, but when someone lingers in it instead of recovers from it, their mourning turns into feelings of hopelessness. Hopelessness is a dangerous emotional state that should be avoided.

The Bible says in Ecclesiastes 3:1-4, "To everything there is a season, a time for every purpose under heaven…A time to weep, and a time to laugh; a time to mourn, and a time to dance."

God's love is unfailing, and He doesn't want us to lose hope during our time of mourning. His Word says, "I do not want you to be ignorant, brethren, concerning those who have fallen asleep [the dead], lest you sorrow as others who have no hope" (1 Thessalonians 4:13). In other words, we should not grieve like those who don't know what their future holds.

The scriptures encourage believers that one day we will be reunited with our loved ones. Our hope is that death is not the end but a brand new beginning in heaven.

To grieve for a moment is expected; however, after sufficient time has passed, we're to gain a proper perspective so that the time of healing can begin, even though there still may be moments of sadness.

Time changes everything. Let me explain. If we were to experience a hurricane today, there would be little to no evidence of the devastation that occurred in a year or two from now because nearly everything would be restored.

In the same way, when we look at pictures of past wars—World War I, World War II, the Korean War, and the Vietnam War—it's apparent that countries, cities, and neighborhoods directly impacted were left decimated. Although mass devastation occurred in those locations in the 1920s, '30s, '40s, and '60s, if we were to visit them today, there would be little to no sign of what took place so long ago. The cities have been completely restored. As a matter of fact, I took a trip a couple of years ago to Germany, and I couldn't believe how beautiful some of the areas were that had previously been ravished by war.

How does one find the path to good grief and good sorrow? It's important to understand that grief is a very personal and sensitive situation. As a pastor, I have consoled thousands of people, and I have found that when individuals experience loss, they seem to go through the process much easier when they feel the presence of peace in their lives rather than distress.

Concerning grief, Arthur Henry Kenney, an Irish priest and Dean of Achonry at the Church of Ireland from 1812 to 1821, stated the following:

> Thanks be to God – that believers do not have to grieve like the world who have no real hope. I really believe if, instead of shutting ourselves into our sorrows and keeping all the light of heaven out of our souls, we opened them to receive Him, Christ would so come to us that the season of our deepest grief and anguish would become one of the richest and most precious of our whole lives.

If you are presently experiencing grief, please know that peace is available to you by simply inviting Jesus, the Prince of Peace, into your circumstances. Furthermore, no matter how great the sadness is in your life, it doesn't have to last. God is faithful to rebuild and restore what you've lost; what the enemy has taken from you.

Joel 2:25 states, "So I will restore to you the years that the swarming locust has eaten, the crawling locust, the consuming locust, and the chewing locust, My great army which I sent among you." As we read this verse, it encourages us to understand that God is able to heal us and restore the lost years that have been devoured by the swarming, crawling and consuming locust.

What do your losses look like? No matter the depth of your loss—the loss of a loved one, the loss of a relationship, a failed marriage, the loss of your health—God is able to restore so that you may reap a harvest. Receive the vine of hope, the tree of life, with genuine courage, to nourish the roots of faith.

As I mentioned, the Lord understands grief and sorrow because He experienced it. We read the following in Isaiah 53:3-5:

> He is despised and rejected by men, a man of sorrows and acquainted with grief. And we hid, as it were, our faces from Him. He was despised, and we did not esteem Him. Surely He has borne our griefs and carried our sorrows; yet we esteemed Him stricken, smitten by God, and afflicted.

> But He was wounded for our transgressions; He was bruised for our iniquities; the chastisement for our peace

was upon Him, and by His stripes we are healed.

What is so amazing about the verse in Isaiah is that it reveals that we no longer have to carry the weight of our sorrows because Jesus already did that for us on the cross. The passage tells us, "By His stripes we are healed." He endured so much for you and me so that we can know and believe there's no situation where Jesus is not enough.

If you don't know how to move from a place of despair, I encourage you to depend on Jesus because He is more than enough. I also challenge you to ask Jesus to heal and restore you by confessing Jeremiah 17:14 (NLT), "O LORD, if you heal me, I will be truly healed; if you save me, I will be truly saved. My praises are for you alone!" And according to Jeremiah 30:17 (NLT), this is the Lord's response to you, "I will give you back your health and heal your wounds."

Here's a question to ask yourself: "When is Jesus not enough for me to be restored?" The answer is NEVER! He is always enough. Do you know why Jesus is enough in the midst of your sorrow and pain? It's because He promises you healing and power, He promises you His presence, and He promises to help you. When the enemy comes and lies to you saying that Jesus isn't enough, you need to tell him that Jesus is more than enough.

ANTIDOTE FOR MOURNING

In biblical times, sackcloth, a fabric usually made of black goat hair, was used to make a covering or a coat. It had a strong odor, and it was not comfortable to wear. It was customary for people to wear sackcloth as a sign of mourning. For example, when Joseph was sold into slavery by his brothers, they went home and told their father Jacob that Joseph had been killed. Because of his grief, Jacob put on sackcloth and went into mourning (Genesis 37:34).

The Bible tells about Nineveh repenting when Jonah came to them, and they put on sackcloth as a sign of repentance (Jonah 3:5-8).

When Mordecai heard of the edict that the king signed to annihilate the Jewish people, he put on sackcloth and went into mourning (Esther 4:1).

The Bible reveals to us that it's okay to grieve, there's an appropriate season when garments are worn to mourn, but at some point we must remove the mourning attire. Unfortunately, many continue to struggle with releasing their mourning garments. They go to the gym, work, the mall, and on vacation dressed in their mourning garments.

When we think about David and Bathsheba, what generally comes to mind is their adulterous relationship. When David learned that Bathsheba was pregnant by him, David sent her husband, Uriah the Hittite, to the front line of a battle to be killed so he could marry Bathsheba. When she gave birth to their baby, the child became ill and died.

We pick up the story in 2 Samuel 12:19 (NIV), "David noticed that his attendants were whispering among themselves, and he realized the child was dead. 'Is the child dead?' he asked. 'Yes,' they replied, 'he is dead.'" David's servants were afraid to tell him what happened.

The next verse reveals how David responded to the news. Verse 20 states:

> Then David got up from the ground. After he had washed, put on lotions and changed his clothes, he went into the house of the LORD and worshiped. Then he went to his own house, and at his request they served him food, and he ate.

Notice David's reaction: He changed his clothes—took off the sackcloth that he was likely wearing—took a bath, and went to the house of the Lord to worship. After he worshiped, he went to his house and requested food. He probably hadn't eaten much in days because his child was gravely ill.

When he asked for food, his servants said to him (2 Samuel 12:21), "Why are you acting this way? While the child was alive, you fasted and wept, but now that the child is dead, you get up and eat!"

The servants were essentially telling David that he was doing the opposite of what most would do under those circumstances. A time of mourning was expected after the child's death, yet David reacted differently.

David answered his servants. According to 2 Samuel 12:22-24, this was his response:

> While the child was still alive, I fasted and wept. I thought, 'Who knows? The Lord may be gracious to

me and let the child live.' But now that he is dead, why should I go on fasting? Can I bring him back again? I will go to him, but he will not return to me.

Then David comforted his wife Bathsheba, and he went to her and made love to her. She gave birth to a son, and they named him Solomon.

I want to focus on a few key points in this story as it relates to grief. First, David was at a place of sorrow, but he didn't stay there. He changed his clothes and put his mourning wear back on the rack. We know that David did not stay there because the Bible tells us that he washed himself, anointed himself, and changed his clothes. He removed himself from the place of grief and began the process of recovery.

Next, David didn't deny the incident, the crisis, the loss because it did happen. He just refused to remain in a state of grief. He did not put his car in park, take off the tires, remove the engine, and behave as if life was over. He kept the engine running. His actions said, "I'm going to be here for a moment, but then I've got to move on."

You may be familiar with the statement: "It's a nice place to visit, but I wouldn't want to live there." Well, some time back, I visited Washington, DC, and it's a nice place to visit, but it's not my cup of tea, and I wouldn't want to live there.

There's also Broken Arrow, Oklahoma, where I went to Bible school. I graduated on a Friday, and the next morning I was moving out of the city, and I haven't been back since. You may wonder if I liked the city. Visiting was fine, but I had no desire to become a permanent resident.

The same should hold true when it comes to sorrow. It's a place we'll all experience, but we're not supposed to be permanent residents.

David's reaction also shows us that he knew how and from whom to get his healing. Notice the progression of what took place. He was sad about his child's illness. Word came to him that the child died. As soon as he heard the news, he picked himself up, took a bath, and changed his clothes. Before he attended to his own home, he went into the house of the Lord to worship. He knew his healing was there. He knew he had to get into the presence of God.

What would be your reaction if you were in a state of mourning? You may not want to pray. You may not want to read your Bible. You may not want to lift your hands and worship God. You may not want to be around Christians or go to church, but that's what you should do. Drag your flesh, by faith, out of your house and into the presence of God. By faith, you pray. By faith, you read the Bible. By faith, you worship God. By faith, you go to church and trust God to change your mourning to joy.

We do many things that we really don't feel like doing, but we must do. I don't always feel like going to work, but I drag my flesh to work. I don't always feel like going to the gym, but I drag my flesh to the gym. Do you ever wake up and think, *Oh, I can't wait to go to the dentist*? Of course not! But what do you do? If it's necessary, you drag your flesh out of the house and go to the dentist.

Consider also how David recognized that before he could

NO MORE SORROW, NO MORE TEARS

comfort his wife, he first had to be whole. He had to allow God to minister to him before he could attend to his wife.

Not every mate takes David's approach to heal and recover after experiencing a loss. As a matter of fact, statistics show that during times of great loss, marriages that once were strong are negatively impacted by the loss. One or both can't handle the grief, so the pair argue or turn on each other.

Keep in mind that David's reaction did not mean he didn't love the child he lost or that the child would be forgotten. A loss of any kind is never simply forgotten.

Years ago, my kidney was removed, and there's a scar where the incision was made. If I press on the scar, I don't feel the pain I once felt, but the scar will always remain.

It's the same with life's scars. We can't take away the scars left behind by life's experiences, but God can supernaturally take away the sting or the pain associated with those scars.

I love the fact that David didn't quit on life. He got back in the game. What do I mean by that? He went home, and he ministered to his wife. We don't know how long it took before her period of grief was over. At some point, though, the garment of praise replaced the spirit of heaviness. Once she was restored, the two of them were able to move on together.

In my rendition of David and Bathsheba's story, I imagine the situation went something like this:

David asked, "Babe, you want to go out for a show

tonight?"

Bathsheba replied, "Oh, sure! We haven't been to a show in a long time."

He said, "I'll also take you to your favorite restaurant; how about that?"

"I'd love that," she replied.

"You look beautiful today," David commented. "I have candy and flowers for you as well."

She smiled and said, "Thank you."

When they returned home from their outing, there were rose petals and silk sheets on the bed. David asked, "What do you think?"

Bathsheba replied, "Oh my goodness; you've thought of everything," and that night, they conceived Solomon.

You can disagree with my interpretation of the scene, but the point is they didn't stop. They pushed past their pain and tried again. They could have decided that the pain of losing a child was too great to try and conceive another. If that had been their decision, they would not have given birth to Solomon, whose name means peace.

Consider what the Word of God says in Isaiah 61:3.

To console those who mourn in Zion, to give them beauty for ashes, the oil of joy for mourning, the garment of praise for the spirit of heaviness; that they may be called trees of righteousness, the planting of the Lord, that He may be glorified.

Although we may experience heartache, the Bible says we'll receive the oil of joy for mourning, beauty for the ashes, and when our hearts are heavy, we'll receive the garment of praise.

I don't know if you watch fighting matches, but I'm kind of a big UFC (Ultimate Fighting Championship) fan. There's a woman who is one of the toughest competitors in the sport. Not long ago, she fought another top competitor and lost the bout. After losing the bout, she became suicidal.

I bring up the story of the UFC competitor to ask this question: So, you can have money, fortune, and fame, and be the poster boy or girl of your profession—you can be on top of the mountain—and then one set back, one attack can take you down a path of no return?

Is life really over after a loss? Of course it isn't, but you have to make up your mind to push past the feelings of hopelessness and find joy.

DON'T STOP

In 2 Samuel 18, we find David experiencing sorrow again as another death occurs in his family—his son Absalom died. When David received word from the battlefield that Absalom died, he was filled with sadness. The Bible reveals the following about David's reaction:

> Then the king was deeply moved, and went up to the chamber over the gate, and wept. And as he went, he said thus: 'O my son Absalom—my son, my son Absalom—if only I had died in your place! O Absalom my son, my son!
>
> —2 Samuel 18:33

The story continues in 2 Samuel 19:1-4:

> Joab was told, 'Behold, the king is weeping and mourning for Absalom.' So the victory that day was turned into mourning for all the people. For the people heard it said that day, 'The king is grieved for his son.' And the people stole back into the city that day, as people who are ashamed steal away when they flee in battle.
>
> But the king covered his face, and the king cried out with a loud voice, 'O my son Absalom! O Absalom, my son, my son!'

The sorrow David felt for Absalom was different from the grief he experienced after losing his child with Bathsheba. David was so distraught that he lost sight of why his army went after Absalom and killed him. The reason being, Absalom rose against his father; he wanted to kill David and take his kingdom. David's men rose to defend his honor, but David didn't believe anything terrible would happen to Absalom. The grief David experienced when Absalom died left him in total despair.

When Joab, the captain of David's army, discovered how David mourned Absalom's death, he went to David and basically told him to get his act together. He told him that his behavior was causing confusion. The people felt ashamed by what took place, that maybe they shouldn't have fought for him, and that maybe Absalom should not have died.

David's reaction sent a strong message to his people after Absalom's death. It was as if his life was no longer worth living. His perpetual grief was becoming destructive. Do you understand why? It's because David lost focus. His focus was no longer on his position as king. He was not reigning during his grieving period. He was neglecting his responsibilities. It was as if he didn't care about his other children, his kingdom, his future, or the call on his life.

Thank God for Joab. We all need Joabs in our lives to come and speak the truth to us. There comes a time when people need to hold our hands and speak encouraging words, and then there comes a time when people need to lift us up out of the place of mourning and say, "Enough is enough!"

Joabs let you know when your actions are becoming destructive. They remind you that others are depending on you. They remind you that there are dreams in your heart and visions for your life. If they recognize the signs, they aren't afraid to tell you that you're headed toward an emotional breakdown and that you'll be stuck in that state for far too long if you don't take action to avoid it.

I make the next statement with compassion and in the best way I can. We cannot afford to allow a person or a possession, whatever and whoever it may be, to have a greater influence in our lives than Jesus Christ. Our love for Christ has to be greater than our love for anyone or anything. When someone says "I can't live without you," or "I can't live without them," whether they realize it or not, they may be on the verge of worshiping that individual.

Jesus said in Matthew 10:37 (NLT), "If you love your father or mother more than you love me, you are not worthy of being mine; or if you love your son or daughter more than me, you are not worthy of being mine."

Know that loving someone is good and healthy. God designed us to love. I believe the verse is saying that the love we have for someone or something should not be greater than our love for Christ. God understands how difficult it is when we lose a loved one or something of value, but we aren't to make them idols of worship where we esteem them greater than the creator of our existence.

Jesus knows us better than we know ourselves, and there may come a day when our love for Him is challenged. With that said, let's look at a story in John 21 (NIV). The passage we'll focus on involves an encounter the disciples had with Jesus after his death and resurrection; it was the third encounter.

Beginning with verse 6, Jesus tells the disciples, "Throw your net on the right side of the boat, and you will find some [fish]." The Bible tells us they caught a "large number of fish." Afterward, Jesus asked them to share some of the fish and have breakfast with Him. The story continues in verse 15.

> When they had finished eating, Jesus said to Simon Peter, 'Simon son of John, do you love me more than these?' 'Yes, Lord,' he said, 'you know that I love you.' Jesus

said, 'Feed my lambs.'

Jesus repeated the question two more times, and both times Peter gave the same answer to which Jesus replied, "Take care of my sheep," "Feed my sheep." Then Jesus spoke the following directly to Peter:

> Very truly I tell you, when you were younger you dressed yourself and went where you wanted; but when you are old you will stretch out your hands, and someone else will dress you and lead you where you do not want to go.' Jesus said this to indicate the kind of death by which Peter would glorify God. Then Jesus said to him, 'Follow me!'
>
> Peter turned and saw that the disciple whom Jesus loved was following them.... When Peter saw him, he asked, 'Lord, what about him?' Jesus answered, 'If I want him to remain alive until I return, what is that to you? You must follow me.'
>
> —John 21:18-22 (NIV)

All too often, people allow the Absaloms and Johns in their lives to distract them or influence their decision to follow Jesus. They get caught up in what others are saying or doing. They feel like someone or something is getting more attention than they are. They don't feel valued. They feel hurt or offended, so they stop going to church, stop praying, and some even stop believing in God.

When Peter questioned Jesus about John, Jesus immediately redirected Peter back to what He asked him to do, "Follow Me." In practical terms, what that means to us is that we can't allow ourselves to get distracted by what God is doing in another person's life. Remember what Jesus said to Peter (verse 22), "What is that to you?" Maintain your perspective! Whatever is happening to someone else is between that person and God. It has nothing to do with the call of God on your life or His love for you.

Keep in mind, when Peter asked Jesus the question, he had no idea that God would use him to touch thousands of people, perform miracles, and become one of the greatest apostles in the early church.

STRENGTHENED AND ENCOURAGED

The sorrow David felt for the first son born to him and Bathsheba and the sorrow he felt for Absalom wasn't unfamiliar to David. 1 Samuel 30 tells of a prior incident that caused David's heart to be filled with sadness. His home was destroyed, and his family was taken captive by his enemy.

> Now it happened when David and his men came to Ziklag on the third day that the Amalekites had invaded the South and Ziklag, and attacked Ziklag and burned it with fire, and had taken captive the women and those who were there, from small to great; they did not kill anyone, but carried them away and went their way.
> —1 Samuel 30:1-2

Ziklag was where David lived with upwards of 600 men (his army) with their wives and possessions. The Amalekites attacked Ziklag when David and his men were away. The story continues in verse 3:

So David and his men came to the city, and there it was, burned with fire; and their wives, their sons, and their daughters had been taken captive. Then David and the people who were with him lifted up their voices and wept, until they had no more power to weep....

Now David was greatly distressed, for the people spoke of stoning him, because the soul of all the people was grieved, every man for his sons and his daughters. But David strengthened himself in the Lord his God....

So David inquired of the Lord, saying, 'Shall I pursue this troop? Shall I overtake them?' And He answered him, 'Pursue, for you shall surely overtake them and without fail recover all.'

—1 Samuel 30:3-8

In this incident, David wore the garment of grief for a brief moment, and then he took it off. While everyone was grieving and everything was chaotic—while there was confusion and drama—notice what David did. The passage tells us, "David strengthened himself in the Lord his God." He put on his new garments: the garment of strength and the garment of courage. They were the garments that would put him in position to recover what the enemy stole.

Here's what we can learn from this story of David: We can't hang around people who are stuck on being sad and expect to be healed. Sometimes we must choose, in love, to turn away from those who will hinder us. We may have to decide not to return the phone call, the text message, lunch or dinner invites because our priority is to be healed. David had to make that choice. He diverted his focus from those who wept to the God who would help him recover all.

Here's another thing to make note of: When people experience tragedies, watch what you say to them. Don't be guilty of holding them back from receiving their healing. If you don't know what to say, just say, "I'm praying for you. How can I help you?" But refrain from asking them what happened, which causes them to relive the tragedy once more.

I know what I'm talking about because it was true for me when I went through cancer treatments. People would come to me and say, "How do you feel?" I would think, *Don't ask me how I feel because you can't help me.* I would have preferred prayer instead of being asked to relive the battles that I had to face at 9:00 a.m., 11:00 a.m., and 1:00 p.m. I wanted to move forward so that I could receive my healing.

It's interesting to read that sometimes Jesus had to take an individual out of their familiar environment for healing to take place. While in Bethsaida, He led a blind man out of the village and healed him (Mark 8:22-26). Could there have been something or someone in the village hindering him from receiving his healing?

Sometimes God does the same thing with you and me. We experience a change in our surroundings because He knows that we can't get healed unless we change our environment.

I have a friend whose wife died. We've been friends for years. During a conversation with him, about seven months after his wife's death, my friend said, "Diego, guess what I did today?"

I asked, "What did you do?"

"I bought brand-new furniture," he replied. "I had to get rid of the old furniture because it represented so many memories. I also cleared out all of my wife's clothes, and I have very limited pictures of her in the house because I have to move on."

I'm not telling you to do the same thing my friend did if you're struggling through a similar situation. What I am telling you is to consider what you're doing or not doing to receive your healing.

Sometimes you have to move items out of the house, store the pictures, and clean out the closet. Sometimes you can't visit the gravesite to honor the memory of your loved one because it holds you back from being restored. Everyone is different, so you must be honest with yourself about what you can handle and what you can't handle.

Furthermore, you must learn how to dream again, and you must learn how to live on by creating new memories, new victories, and new experiences. I'm not saying you have to forget the past, but I am asking you to remember God in the midst of your situation.

Something else to consider; you may want to help someone else in need to take your mind off yourself. It's all a part of the healing process.

There's a condition called "broken heart syndrome." It's experienced when one mate dies and, shortly thereafter, the other mate dies. The second mate to pass may have been in perfect health but the stress of losing a spouse produced heart fatigue which resulted in heart failure and death. It may have happened to a couple you know, or you may have heard about a couple in the public arena.

Doug Flutie, a former NFL quarterback, lost his dad, and one day later, his mom died. There was a famous actress named Mary Tamm who was married to Marcus Ringnose. Marcus gave the eulogy for Mary Tamm, and the next day, he died.

People who lose hope feel they have no purpose. Sadly, they don't recognize that God has something more for them.

When David lost Absalom, he didn't continue in a state of grief for a prolonged period or lose hope. Instead, he did what should have been done. He strengthened and encouraged himself in the Lord.

David was a premium worshiper. He carried a harp on his hip, and he wrote many of the Psalms of worship in the Bible. In Psalm 34, David wrote, "I will bless the Lord at all times. His praise shall continually be in my mouth."

I imagine David picking up the harp, after Absalom's death, and saying, *"I'm going to take off the garment of mourning and put on the garment of praise. I don't feel like it, but I'm going to do it by faith."*

We see in Jude 1:20 another way to encourage oneself. It says, "But you, beloved, building yourselves up on your most holy faith, praying in the Holy Spirit...."

Pray in the Spirit because sometimes your flesh doesn't want to pray or you don't know what to say. Sometimes you don't have the emotional strength to pray in your understanding, so pray in the Spirit with the help of the Holy Spirit.

I'm an advocate of praying in the Spirit. I also recognize not everyone believes in praying in the Spirit. My life, however, has been established on this belief over the last 37 years of my Christian faith. I went through some of the most hellish days in my life during my bout with cancer. I can't imagine enduring what I had to endure without the ability to pray in the Spirit. I don't know how I would have made it through some of those days. I'll admit, there were days I had to dig down deep inside to find the strength to pray.

One of my favorite verses on prayer is found in Romans 8:26, which states, "Likewise the Spirit helps us in our weakness. For we do not know what we should pray for as we ought, but the Spirit Himself makes intercession for us with groanings which cannot be uttered."

When we don't know how or what to say what's on our hearts, when we pray in the Spirit, in faith, the Spirit appeals to God on our behalf.

You should also encourage yourself by confessing the Word of God over your life. Reciting the following scriptures was a part of my regular routine:

> "I shall not die, but live, and declare the works of the Lord."
>
> —Psalm 118:17

"All things work together for good to those who love God, to those who are the called according to His purpose."
—Romans 8:28

"I will restore health to you and heal you of your wounds...."
—Jeremiah 30:17

It's important to confess the Word of God over your life. I recommend that you commit as many scriptures as you can to memory. Hebrews 10:23 states, "Let us hold fast the confession of our hope without wavering, for He who promised is faithful."

I want to share an astonishing story about a man named Horatio Spafford who lived in the 1800s. He was a devout Christian who understood the importance of taking off the garment of mourning.

Horatio resided in Chicago. He was a very successful lawyer, a real estate investor, and a good man. He was married and had five children—one son and four daughters.

In the late 1860s, Horatio's son died. In 1871, the year of the great Chicago fire, he lost his business and all his real estate investments as a result of the fire.

While trying to recover from the losses he endured, he thought he'd send his family on vacation. He was delayed due to business transactions, so he put his wife and four daughters on a ship, kissed them goodbye, and sent them to Europe. His plan was to join them not long after their departure.

In the middle of the Atlantic, the ship collided with another vessel. All four daughters drowned in the ocean. Horatio received a telegram from his wife that stated, "I alone am saved."

Not long after Horatio received notice of what took place, he boarded a ship to go and comfort his wife. During his journey, the captain brought him forward and said, "We believe this is the area where your daughters drowned when the vessels collided." At that moment, Horatio took a piece of paper and began to pen the words of a song.

Years passed, and he and his wife had three more children—two girls and a boy. Sadly, that son died as well.

Horatio Spafford experienced much tragedy during his life. But the words of the song he wrote in 1873, as he stood on the ship overlooking the place where his four daughters drowned, reveal to us how he dealt with sorrow. The following are the lyrics to Horatio's song, "It Is Well with My Soul":

When peace like a river, attendeth my way,
When sorrows like sea billows roll;
Whatever my lot, thou hast taught me to know,
It is well; it is well, with my soul.

Refrain:
It is well with my soul,
It is well; it is well with my soul.

Though Satan should buffet, though trials should come,
Let this blest assurance control,
That Christ has regarded my helpless estate,
And hath shed His own blood for my soul.

My sin, oh, the bliss of this glorious thought!
My sin, not in part but the whole,
Is nailed to the cross, and I bear it no more,
Praise the Lord, praise the Lord, O my soul.

For me, be it Christ, be it Christ hence to live:
If Jordan above me shall roll,
No pang shall be mine, for in death as in life
Thou wilt whisper Thy peace to my soul!

But, Lord, 'tis for Thee, for Thy coming we wait,
The sky, not the grave, is our goal;
Oh, trump of the angel! Oh, voice of the Lord!
Blessed hope, blessed rest of my soul!

And Lord, haste the day when my faith shall be sight,
The clouds be rolled back as a scroll;
The trump shall resound, and the Lord shall descend,
A song in the night, oh my soul!

Whatever you are facing today, or when you come face to face with sadness and grief, sing this song or read the lyrics, especially when you feel that sorrow is getting the best of you. Horatio Spafford wrote these words from his heart as he viewed the place where his daughters died. Like Horatio, when you turn to Jesus, who is more than enough for any situation, for any sorrow, for immeasurable grief, it will be well with your soul.

If you're sad about something that occurred in your life, God would want you to let it go and give it to Him. Let there be no more sorrow and no more tears. Allow God to lift the garment of mourning and replace it with the garments of faith, hope, and love. It's time to heal, it's time to laugh, it's time to dance, and it's time to plant new dreams and experience a bright future.

To help you through your sorrow, consider writing a letter to someone, something, or to yourself to bring closure. You may be experiencing grief due to a broken friendship, loss of a job, the sale of a cherished home, or a breakup with the love of your life. Expressing your feelings in writing may prove to be beneficial and liberating.

In addition, as difficult as it may seem, remember to celebrate the good times, be grateful, love, forgive, bless those who hurt you, and move on.

Lastly, Dr. Henry Cloud, a clinical psychologist and top-selling author, has two books I believe would make good reading on this subject: *Necessary Endings* and *Boundaries*.

Prayer

Father, in the name of Jesus, I release my mourning, my grieving, my sadness today, that which has been prolonged. Father, whether I'm stuck in a season or a moment, I release it to You now so that I can move forward. I know that my life is not over.

In the name of Jesus, I pray that undue grief and the spirit of heaviness be lifted off of me. Like chains that have bound me, may they be shaken off, in the name of Jesus. Impart in me new dreams and new visions, God, so that I can move forward from the place of sackcloth and ashes.

Father, may I grab hold of Your hand, and may You walk me through this valley of the shadow of death and bring me to the other side. You promised me joy, and You promised me peace. Today, I take off this sorrow and put on the garment of praise.

I now live to glorify you, God. I will walk in the calling you've placed upon my life. I ask You to heal my broken and grieving heart now. Thank You, Holy Spirit.

In Jesus' name. Amen.

Questions

Jesus knows what it's like to be human. He understands our weaknesses and temptations according to Hebrews 4:15-16. How can you console someone who is facing a loss, using Jesus as an example?

_____

_____

_____

_____

If you've lost a loved one, how did the people around you support you as you went through the grieving process? Were they helpful or harmful?

_____

_____

_____

_____

Explain the differences in how David grieved after the loss of the son born to him and Bathsheba and the loss of his son Absalom. Have you experienced such extremes? Explain.

_____

_____

_____

_____

Sometimes we may need to remove ourselves from people, places, and things to receive complete healing after a devastating loss. Have you experienced that in your life? Explain.

_____

_____

_____

_____

Additional Notes:

_____

_____

_____

_____

CHAPTER 7

AVOID ANGER

"Anger is an acid that can do more harm to the vessel in which it is stored than to anything on which it is poured."

—*Mark Twain*

Consider the statement above made by Mark Twain. Notice that he described anger as an acid. Acid is corrosive. When an acid comes in contact with a substance, it eats away at it. Acid has the potential to dissolve a thing altogether.

In situations where acid is involved, it's crucial to regard the warnings, use proper equipment, and neutralize spills immediately.

The same precautions regarded for acids should be taken where anger is involved. We should notice the warning signs, be equipped to handle or confront them, and neutralize outbursts at the onset.

What has been your experience with anger? Has anger ever damaged a connection (relationship) that you valued?

Over the years, I've learned of many relationships damaged by anger. More often than not, the damage caused could have been avoided.

You may be familiar with the phrase, "Hindsight is 20/20." That simply implies that it's easy to see the effects of one's actions after the fact. That certainly is true, but does it have to be lived out in every situation we encounter? It does not! In many instances, we need only to consider the consequences before we act.

A situation that may cause one to become angry at another is a situation that calls for those involved to consider the consequences. If there is a less damaging alternative, why not utilize that approach?

Some would say that considering the consequences before acting out in anger is easier said than done. I would counter that statement with a question: What's more manageable, mending a broken bond or protecting a solid one?

When a bond is broken, there are often fragments (trust, loyalty, respect, attraction) that are never recovered. Unfortunately, what was broken may never be the same. I believe in protecting what I value. There's no need to recover what was never severed or lost.

In this chapter, you'll learn about the pain that anger produces and how the agony endured can harm not only the individual harboring the anger but anything and everyone involved. You'll learn what triggers anger as well as solutions to overcome triggers. You'll also discover what the Word of God has to say about this destructive emotion.

Humor is disbursed throughout the chapter to lighten the subject matter.

Know that you don't have to live with anger. It can be avoided.

WHAT'S FUELING THE RAGE?

Take a close look at the word anger. Did you notice that it is one letter away from the word danger? That's fitting because when you get to the place where your blood is boiling, your temperature is rising, and you feel like cursing and spitting at the same time, that's a dangerous place for you and others.

What if individuals who are prone to anger realized they are in charge of that emotion? In other words, they are the ones controlling the anger they display, not someone or something else. Maybe many would see that they've been angry too long. Perhaps they would realize that they've been blaming the wrong person for what they feel.

Some people give control to someone or something else, enabling the negative emotion to manifest. Control may be granted purposefully or ignorantly. An example of purposefully granting authority would be to intentionally allow someone or something to draw out the emotion that would likely lie dormant. For example, some consume mood-altering substances to become someone they aren't usually.

An example of ignorantly granting authority to someone or something would be when an unresolved offense evolves into anger because it wasn't dealt with at the onset. Although unintended, issues remain issues without resolution. Matthew 18:15 (NIV) tells us, "Go privately and point out the offense."

In 1982, *Blade Runner,* a science fiction thriller, was released. Harrison Ford played the leading role as Detective Rick Deckard.

As a detective, Deckard's job was to identify and terminate humanoid robots that escaped space colonies and returned to Earth. The robots were so advanced that they displayed emotions, including anger. In the movie, Detective Deckard found himself running for his life from angry, out-of-control robots that began hunting him. The robots were so blinded by hate and rage that they focused on one objective—destroy Detective Deckard.

Like most movies, the hero escaped, and the bad guys lost. The robots' power source was short-circuited, which caused their battery to drain.

I sometimes wonder how life would change if negative emotions had an off/on switch or an expiration date. It's likely fewer people would need medication, therapy, or mood-altering substances to counteract negative emotions' adverse effects.

Although it would resolve many problems, there is no expiration date on anger. It doesn't just vanish at the close of day. Anger can arise with you when you wake up in the morning if you fail to put it out the night before.

Anger can begin with a morning disappointment that turned

into mid-morning resentment that turned into a noonday offense that turned into late afternoon unforgiveness that turned into early evening strife, which ended up as full-blown rage. During the day, you nursed the disappointment; you nourished it and coddled it like a baby. By evening, it's fully embraced and drawn close to your heart.

I believe the moment we feel like blowing up in anger, we should short circuit what's fueling that emotion. We should detach from the source. We should disconnect from the negative energy, unplug from the shock potential, pull the plug that's charging the battery. I believe you get the picture.

Anger can be traced to issues in your past that were never resolved, such as daddy issues, abandonment, rejection, abuse, or bullying. It may involve closure you never received or forgiveness you never offered.

Maybe you had a bad relationship with your mother or father. Perhaps you were unjustly treated as a child. Perhaps you experienced some form of failure or made a major mistake that set you in a low place in life. Over time, those unresolved issues surfaced in the form of anger.

Anger may be an issue for you because you've gotten away with it for too long. You may even use it as a means to keep people at a distance. If no one ever confronted you about it, it will continue to be your issue. That may be hard to believe about yourself, but it's the truth.

I remember several occasions when I felt a strong rebuke from the Holy Spirit about being angry. Having stage 4, terminal kidney cancer in 2008 is related to a few cases. That was a weary season in my life, and mainly due to how I felt.

There were times when I got mad because of how long it took for my healing to manifest. I would even take it out on my dogs by yelling at them, pulling the leash hard when they wouldn't listen, and even, I'm sorry to say, kicking them when they didn't obey.

I would take my frustration out on people I didn't know. For example, if someone cut me off when I was driving, I'd get mad and say a few choice words.

Those close to me were also in direct line of fire. If a staff member failed at his or her job, I'd raise my voice toward them. I was very short-tempered with my wife if she forgot something I asked her to do.

A walking time bomb with a very short fuse is what I was. I was a volcano ready to irrupt; a Sherman tank prepared to roll over anyone in my path.

We can try to justify and excuse the anger we display, but, again, it's a choice, and we must take responsibility for it. Directing anger upon the innocent instead of focusing on resolving the problem is pointless. It's not helping anyone involved. Failing to deal with an issue creates frustration which gives rise to an offense.

You have the power. Don't allow an issue to get under your skin. Deal with it, then shake off negative emotions like dust.

ANGER AWARENESS

Anger & Exasperation

A young girl who was writing a paper for school came to her father and asked: "Dad, what is the difference between anger and exasperation?"

The father replied: "It is mostly a matter of degree. Let me show you what I mean."

With that, the father went to the telephone and dialed a random number. To the man who answered the phone, he said: "Hello, is Melvin there?"

The man answered: "There is no one living here named Melvin. Why don't you learn to look up numbers before you dial."

"See," said the father to his daughter. "That man was not a bit happy with our call. He was probably very busy with something, and we annoyed him. Now watch." The father dialed the number again.

"Hello, is Melvin there?" asked the father.

"Now look here!" came the heated reply. "You just called this number, and I told you that there is no Melvin here! You've got a lot of guts calling again!" The receiver slammed down hard.

The father turned to his daughter and said: "You see, that

was anger. Now I'll show you what exasperation means."

He dialed the same number, and when a violent voice roared: "Hello!" The father calmly said: "Hello, this is Melvin. Have there been any calls for me?"

(https://upjoke.com)

Have you ever struck out in anger against someone and regretted it? Have you ever acted out in rage repeatedly? Have you ever reacted in anger because someone opposed you? In Numbers 22, we can read the story about Balaam—a prophet who lacked discernment. He responded in anger when a situation didn't go the way he anticipated.

Balaam was traveling on a donkey to do something he was not supposed to do—curse God's people rather than bless them. A king hired him to pronounce bad things on God's people. In Numbers 22:22-28, we read the following:

Then God's anger was aroused because he went, and the Angel of the Lord took His stand in the way as an adversary against him. And he was riding on his donkey, and his two servants were with him.

Now the donkey saw the Angel of the Lord standing in the way with His drawn sword in His hand, and the donkey turned aside out of the way and went into the field. So Balaam struck the donkey to turn her back onto the road. Then the Angel of the Lord stood in a narrow path between the vineyards, with a wall on this side and a wall on that side. And when the donkey saw the Angel of the Lord, she pushed herself against the wall and crushed

Balaam's foot against the wall; so he struck her again. Then the Angel of the Lord went farther, and stood in a narrow place where there was no way to turn either to the right hand or to the left. And when the donkey saw the Angel of the Lord, she lay down under Balaam; so Balaam's anger was aroused, and he struck the donkey with his staff.

Then the Lord opened the mouth of the donkey, and she said to Balaam, 'What have I done to you, that you have struck me these three times?'

God caused the donkey to stop Balaam from moving forward to carry out the king's request. The donkey saw a barrier—something or someone stopping her—and tried to stop Balaam. Balaam, however, in his anger, struck the donkey three times because of its actions.

Oftentimes, like Balaam, we take our anger out in the wrong way and against the wrong people. The donkey was trying to keep Balaam and herself out of danger. She was trying to help him, not harm him.

You're probably familiar with the phrase, "Strike three; you're out!" Well, for Balaam, his three strikes, out of anger, harmed an innocent animal. His three strikes caused him to be confronted by God.

Why was Balaam angry? What caused that negative emotion to overtake him? He was acting out of the will of God and performing his will in the situation. He was going in the wrong direction, although he believed he was doing what was right.

What can be learned from Balaam and his instance of anger? First, after the initial strike in anger, we should swiftly repent so there is no repeat occurrence. And, we should do what God wants us to do, and we'll have peace. When we decide to go against what God wants, it's just a matter of time before we're confronted. Hopefully, we choose to do it God's way before it's too late.

The Angel who stopped the donkey explained the situation to Balaam. In verse 33, we read, "The donkey saw Me and turned aside from Me these three times. If she had not turned aside from Me, surely I would also have killed you by now, and let her live."

Some choose to ignore the warnings that come from others, and the consequences can be great. The Bible tells us in Proverbs 11:14 (AMP), "Where there is no [wise, intelligent] guidance, the people fall [and go off course like a ship without a helm], but in the abundance of [wise and godly] counselors there is victory."

In Balaam's situation, his means of transportation became the agent God used to keep him from harm. It's important to recognize the difference between what or who is carrying you toward danger and what or who is trying to prevent your downfall.

Angry people typically don't think they have an anger problem. Most people don't recognize their issues until someone points them out or their anger takes them someplace it shouldn't. Unfortunately, such situations often result in losses and unfortunate victims. Even then, many don't accept their faults or acknowledge criticism immediately.

Accepting a person's negative perception of you is not easy. Many disguise their acceptance by rationalizing or justifying their behavior. It's difficult to rid yourself of perfectionism, pride, ignorance, and arrogance when you're living in denial.

You've probably said or heard someone say, "I lost my temper." Well, if it's lost, don't search for it. Allow it to remain lost—far from you and others. That's meant to be humorous, but there is truth in it. If something is lost, it cannot be transferred to others. Instead of giving someone a piece of your mind, place that piece in the valley of lost and forgotten objects and choose not to retrieve it.

When the Apostle Paul said, "Be ye angry, and sin not." (Ephesians 4:26 KJV), he referenced King David's words in Psalm 4:4. Based on this verse, it's assumed that people will get angry. Although anger does not place us in the best light, it happens. How we deal with it if it festers, heats up, boils, and cooks is the true test of our Christian character.

It's implied in Ephesians 4:26 that we can choose to sin or not sin when anger arises. Everyone gets irritated, insulted, and ticked off, but an irritation can rise in degree—like leaven in bread—if it's not confronted quickly.

As previously stated, when anger arises, it can be dangerous for you and others. Realize that in the presence of danger, sin is likely lurking nearby. Maybe that's why the Bible encourages us to resolve, on the same day, an issue that causes us to be angry (Ephesians 4:26-27).

In the Jewish culture, the start of a day is not sunrise but sunset because you will never have a good night's sleep if a situation or event makes you restless. It would be best if you settled a matter quickly. It's most beneficial to resolve it, let it go, and give it to God sooner than later.

Everyone gets angry or frustrated, but where your emotions take you and how long they keep you is what matters. The overall effect emotions have on you—what they make you do—determines whether your behavior is acceptable or detrimental.

KNOW YOUR TRIGGERS

<u>What You Don't Know…</u>

Husband: "When I get mad at you, you never fight back. How do you control your anger?"
Wife: "I clean the toilet."
Husband: "How does that help?"
Wife: "I use your toothbrush."

(https://upjoke.com)

Knowing the buttons that ignite anger within you is crucial. Depending on how long anger has been an issue, it may have evolved into a habit that you've grown accustomed to incorporating in nearly every response. It has become a part of your personality or lifestyle. Even then, it's a choice reaction, although it's done without thinking. It's second nature, but you can choose to change.

During that weary season in my life, as I battled cancer, I allowed my tiredness and disappointment to take me to a place that wasn't attractive. My attitude was similar to the child you see at the mall or in the restaurant who throws a temper tantrum because he didn't get his way. He pouts, screams, hits, throws things, falls to the ground, throws his head back, and may even say mean things.

Maybe you can identify with this behavior. Perhaps you see yourself—an adult behaving like an angry child who hits, throws things, says bad words, hides under the bed, or shows a mean face.

Recognize and avoid childish responses. 1 Corinthians 13:11 reminds us to "Put away childish things." Proverbs 19:11 (NLT) states, "Sensible people control their temper; they earn respect by overlooking wrongs."

No matter the age, a temper tantrum is never pleasant. Children, as well as adults, need to be told what is and is not acceptable behavior.

The key to cutting anger off before it progresses is addressing it, setting boundaries, and being consistent. People need to know there are consequences for their behavior. Remember, anger in and of itself is not a sin. It's what occurs when anger goes unchecked that may result in sin.

An initial step in the deliverance process is being self-aware and acknowledging the problem rather than denying it. The following are a few questions to ask yourself to get to the root cause of the issue.

- If you have an anger issue, what would you say is the cause? Why do you get angry?

- In what situations are you consistently angry? Where do you get angry (place or season)?

- Do you think it's a controlled or uncontrolled anger?

- Do you believe you can still act Christ-like when you become angry?

- Who or what are your triggers; what sets you off?

If you answered these questions truthfully, thank you for your honesty.

I feel that I'm the type of person who can take a little abuse, neglect, mocking, or joking. However, my trigger—what used to set me off—was when someone cursed at me.

Not that it happened all the time, but there have been occasions, in my past, when someone spoke distasteful words in anger toward me. In those moments, my rage meter would go from zero to ten in a matter of seconds. It wasn't pretty. Just joking…maybe. Over time, however, I learned to recognize and be ready for when similar situations were on the rise. Rather than lash out in anger by stating a few expletives of my own, I now maintain control.

ANGER MANAGEMENT

Three Wishes

One day, a man was walking along the beach when he

tripped over a lamp. He turned around and kicked the lamp out of anger. A few seconds later, a genie popped out of the lamp.

Reluctantly, the genie said, "Even though you kicked me, I still have to give you three wishes. However, because of what you did, I will also give twice what you wish for to the person you hate the most: your boss."

The man agreed and made his first wish. "I want lots of money," he said.

Instantly, 22 million dollars appeared in the man's bank account, and 44 million appeared in his boss's account.

For his second wish, the man requested a few sports cars. Instantly, a Lamborghini, Ferrari, and Porsche appeared. At the same time, two of each of those cars appeared outside of his boss's house.

Finally, the genie said, "This is your last wish; you should choose carefully."

To this, the man replied, "I've always wanted to donate a kidney."

(https://jokojokes.com)

Anger can be viewed as a selfish desire to be in control. Some people don't like to wait for anything, and when things don't move as quickly as they expect, they become extremely irritated, and anger arises. It could be seen when someone doesn't respond as soon as they like to a text, email, or voicemail.

Some like being in charge of everything, and sometimes that can't happen, so they get angry. An example would be when someone cuts in front of another driver on the highway or throws a one-finger peace sign, and they allow road rage to come over them. It could be seen when someone doesn't get their menu order right, so they respond in an unbecoming way.

Have you ever had someone not react the way you thought they should? Did you take it as an insult and become angry? In 1 Kings 21, you can read about a king who fits this general description.

King Ahab, the King of Israel during that time, tried to buy a parcel of land owned by a man named Naboth. Naboth didn't want to sell his land because it was a family inheritance. Because Ahab didn't get his way, he became angry. In 1 Kings 21:2-4 (NIV), we read the following:

> Ahab said to Naboth, 'Let me have your vineyard to use for a vegetable garden, since it is close to my palace. In exchange I will give you a better vineyard or, if you prefer, I will pay you whatever it is worth.' But Naboth replied, 'The Lord forbid that I should give you the inheritance of my ancestors.'

> So Ahab went home, sullen and angry because Naboth the Jezreelite had said, 'I will not give you the inheritance of my ancestors.' He lay on his bed sulking and refused to eat.

There's a message in Naboth's decision—we sell things off too quickly; we don't hold onto things of value; we sell out too quickly—but that's for another time. Let's get back to the situation involving Ahab.

Remember the example of the angry child? Does that sound like Ahab? He was a man with authority—the King of Israel. He had land but desired the land owned by someone else. When his proposal was rejected, the Bible says (verse 4), "Ahab went home, sullen and angry." It also reveals he laid on his bed and began to sulk. Wow! What a vivid illustration of an adult behaving childishly.

The passage tells us that Ahab explained to his wife the reason he was angry. Let's take a look at verses 5-6.

> His wife Jezebel came in and asked him, 'Why are you so sullen? Why won't you eat?' He answered her, 'Because I said to Naboth the Jezreelite, Sell me your vineyard; or if you prefer, I will give you another vineyard in its place. But he said, "I will not give you my vineyard.'

Notice the difference between what Naboth stated as the reason and what Ahab told his wife. Naboth said (verse 3), "The Lord forbid that I should give you the *inheritance* of my ancestors." Ahab told Jezebel that Naboth said, "I will not give you my vineyard."

Anger will have you tell half-truths and leave out vital information to get your way. For example, notice that Ahab left out the part when Naboth explained that it was an inheritance. It was land passed down from generation to generation. It was a valuable piece of property that he likely intended to pass down to future generations.

In his mind, what Ahab wanted was more important than what Naboth wanted, but what Ahab wanted wasn't his to possess.

One of the Ten Commandments states that we are not to covet (desire to possess) anything that belongs to our neighbor. As the King of Israel, it's highly likely that Ahab was well versed in the Commandments. However, based on his actions, he didn't consider the Commandments; his desire was greater.

When Naboth refused Ahab's proposal, Ahab should have walked away and accepted the decision. However, he couldn't accept it with a pure heart which is why anger developed.

Rejection and disappointment are a part of life. We can have the greatest expectations but not live them out. Don't be moved or become angry, but move on to something else. Don't force or abuse your authority like Ahab.

Accept that you won't always get your way. Don't get angry. Accept that some things aren't meant for you to have, at least not now. Accept other people's right to hold onto what they have, even their opinions, but don't get angry. Accept that you're not the boss, in charge, or calling *all* the shots, but don't get mad. Accept that some things may not change or get better, but don't get angry. Realize that your anger can hurt or destroy people and that there are consequences for your actions.

Another thing to note is that Ahab involved someone who would likely side with him. He told his wife Jezebel, who had a great deal of influence.

It's one thing to err; it's another thing to recruit cosigners for your errors.

By telling his wife a half-truth, by sulking and feeling as if he was deprived of what was rightfully his, Ahab pulled in someone who got caught up in a mess. It was a mess that would eventually yield a terrible outcome.

Verses 7-10 tell us that Jezebel plotted to have Naboth killed to acquire his land for Ahab. Verses 13-15 reveal that her endeavor was a success. However, there would be consequences for what was done. In verses 17-19 (NIV), we read the following:

> Then the word of the Lord came to Elijah the Tishbite: "Go down to meet Ahab king of Israel, who rules in Samaria. He is now in Naboth's vineyard, where he has gone to take possession of it. Say to him, 'This is what the Lord says: Have you not murdered a man and seized his property?' Then say to him, 'This is what the Lord says: In the place where dogs licked up Naboth's blood, dogs will lick up your blood—yes, yours!'"

God got involved, and what Ahab considered a victory resulted in his undoing. 1 Kings 22:34-38 tells us that Ahab died just as it was said to him by Elijah. Jezebel didn't escape retribution. You can read about her death in 2 Kings 9.

Anger is a negative emotion that can rob you of your future. The Bible tells of many people who had anger issues. I encourage you to take time to read their stories and learn from them so that you don't follow the path they took, which, oftentimes, didn't end well. The following are just a few biblical instances:

- Cain's anger problem caused him to kill his brother Abel. (Genesis 4:8-9) You don't want that.

- Naaman became angry when he was told what he had to do to be healed of leprosy. (2 King 5:10-12) You don't want that.

- Sanballat and Tobiah were angry over Nehemiah rebuilding Jerusalem's wall that left them as nonparticipants with no inheritance. (Nehemiah 4:7) You definitely don't want that!

- Moses' anger caused him to hit the rock, but God told him to speak to the rock. His actions stopped him from entering his promised land of rest. (Numbers 20:7-12) You don't want that.

- King Saul was angry that David got more attention than he did, so he tried to hurt David. His actions destroyed their relationship. (1 Samuel 18) Nope, that's not for me.

- King Herod was angry over the birth of Jesus to the point that he murdered children. (Matthew 2:16-18) That's never a good thing.

- Haman became angry when Mordecai would not bow to him. Haman was hung while Mordecai took his place of honor. (Esther 3:5; 7:10) It's not worth it.

- The disciples of Jesus were angry over a woman breaking a costly alabaster jar of perfume and pouring it out on Jesus. (Mark 14:3-9) Don't want that!

RIGHTEOUS ANGER

Highway Hitchhiker

A man is driving down a highway when he sees a priest hitchhiking. So, being a good Catholic, he picks him up. They drive a bit farther down the highway when the man then spots a well-known lawyer hitchhiking as well. Remembering that the lawyer represented his ex-wife during their divorce, an impulse of anger caused him to aim his car right at the lawyer. He then recalls the priest in his car, and at the last minute, swerves to miss him. The man then turns to the priest and says, "Father, forgive me, I nearly hit that lawyer!"

The priest responds, "Don't worry, my son, I got him with the door!"

(https://upjoke.com)

There are occasions when anger can be a good thing; however, defining and understanding good (righteous) anger is essential.

Good anger motivates us to act when we hear untruths or witness the unjust treatment of others. Human trafficking, underserved communities, homelessness, and child abuse deserve the world's attention and should provoke us to do something to help make a positive change. Good anger is also sinless. It doesn't place others in harm's way.

Unlike good anger, bad anger disrupts our lives, controls our thoughts, and ruins relationships. Destructive anger causes pain and must be avoided.

Keep in mind that even good anger can morph into bad anger. Showing hatred toward someone or wanting bad things to happen to someone because of how others are unjustly treated is bad anger.

James 1:19-20 (NIV) says, "My dear brothers and sisters, take note of this: Everyone should be quick to listen, slow to speak and slow to become angry, because human anger does not produce the righteousness that God desires."

Know when you're about to cross the line and turn back. Don't choose destruction or violence. Take control of your emotions and recognize the difference between destructive and constructive behavior.

In Matthew 21:12-13 (NIV), we read the story of Jesus, who became angry over the money changers selling at the temple, defying and disrespecting God's house. That was righteous anger on display. He said to them, "It is written, 'My house will be called a house of prayer,' but you are making it 'a den of robbers.'"

Jesus was angry that people turned sin into an ordinary affair and profited from it in God's house. There was abuse, misuse, and extortion when it came to selling and sacrificing animals. Money-hungry people were manipulating a system to take advantage of people to gain personal wealth.

To be angry at what makes God angry is righteous anger. It is stirred up by sin that perverts God's goodness. God's Word governs righteous anger.

Jesus said, "If you love me, you will keep my commandments." The most familiar commandments are the Ten Commandments, which are meant to guide people's lifestyles. They are found in the book of Exodus in the Bible's Old Testament. In addition to the Ten Commandments, there are many other commandments found in the Word of God. I encourage you to study the subject of "God's Commands" to develop knowledge and a better understanding of God's Word.

Growing in the grace of righteous anger is a process. It's a part of being conformed and transformed to the image of Christ (Romans 8:29). That may look like learning to hate sin, having a disdain for disobedience, scorning injustice and unrighteousness, or detesting corruption, evil, and deception. But, remember, your response should not resemble human anger because that does not produce the righteousness desired by God.

TAKE ACTION AGAINST ANGER

Results Matter

A priest and a taxi driver arrive at the pearly gates. St. Peter welcomes them and shows them to their homes. For the taxi driver, there's a beautiful villa overlooking a gorgeous field of clouds.

"Thank you," the ecstatic taxi driver said.

Anticipating an even bigger mansion, the priest was dismayed when he arrived at a small 1-bedroom apartment.

"St. Peter, I'm a little puzzled," the priest began. "As a clergyman, I devoted decades of my life solely to serving the Lord. How come the taxi driver got a villa, and for me, only a small apartment?"

St. Peter smiled. "Up here, we go by results. While you preached, people slept; while he drove, people prayed."

(https://upjoke.com)

In Romans 12:2, we read, "And do not be conformed to this world, but be transformed by the renewing of your mind, that you may prove what is that good and acceptable and perfect will of God."

I want you to know that no matter how long you've struggled with anger, no matter how serious your situation is, God desires that you be set free. Even if you feel or believe it's impossible, know that with God, all things are possible (Matthew 19:26).

Confess God's Word and put it into action. Doing so can change you. The following scriptures are an excellent place to start as you begin a lifestyle of confessing God's Word. As you confess His Word, believe God for healing and deliverance.

"Search me, O God, and know my heart! Try me and know my thoughts! And see if there be any grievous way in me, and lead me in the way everlasting!"
—Psalm 139:23-24 (ESV)

"And I will give you a new heart, and a new spirit I will put within you. And I will remove the heart of stone from your flesh and give you a heart of flesh."
—Ezekiel 36:26 (ESV)

"Create in me a clean heart, O God, and renew a right spirit within me."

—Psalm 51:10 (ESV)

"Better a patient person than a warrior, one with self-control than one who takes a city."

—Proverbs 16:32 (NIV)

"Refrain from anger and turn from wrath; do not fret—it leads only to evil."

—Psalm 37:8 (NIV)

"A person's wisdom yields patience; it is to one's glory to overlook an offense."

—Proverbs 19:11 (NIV)

"Do not make friends with a hot-tempered person, do not associate with one easily angered."

—Proverbs 22:24 (NIV)

"Anger is cruel and fury overwhelming, but who can stand before jealousy?"

—Proverbs 27:4 (NIV)

"But now you must also rid yourselves of all such things as these: anger, rage, malice, slander, and filthy language from your lips."

—Colossians 3:8 (NIV)

"Everyone should be quick to listen, slow to speak and slow to become angry, because human anger does not produce the righteousness that God desires."

—James 1:19 (NIV)

"For if you forgive others their trespasses, your heavenly Father will also forgive you, but if you do not forgive others their trespasses, neither will your Father forgive your trespasses."

—Matthew 6:14-15 (ESV)

In the same way that physical exercise can lead to profound changes in the body, so can a daily regimen that involves the Word of God. It can produce astonishing results in your spirit, soul, and body. The Word of God is calming, soothing, and it effectively heals.

It's time to get rid of the negative emotions that cause you to be spiritually sluggish and flabby. Commit to building your spiritual muscles through the Word of God, and become strong in your emotions. I suggest searching for scriptures that speak of God's love, peace, strength, and patience.

Dedication and commitment to daily spiritual transformation can heal a wounded spirit and set one free from the negativity related to anger. It also makes way for a deeper relationship with God and His Word, which results in a better understanding of God's absolute love, care, and concern for you.

Consider the following when confronted with anger. It can make a world of difference for you and those around you.

- Take a time out. Count to ten and take deep breaths.

- Walk away and think about the best way to respond or interpret the situation correctly.

- Change the station in your mind by thinking about something else. Focus on someone or something you love (your happy place).

- Consider the consequences of negative behavior; how things may turn out if not handled properly (the losses).

- Go on a walk or run; exert energy to relieve the tension (the release switch).

- Pray about the situation and give it to God (trust and rest).

- Meditate on God's Word. Search for scriptures that can guide you toward resolution and combat a negative mindset.

- Ask God to reveal why you become angry. Learn your triggers and get to the root. Develop your discernment.

- Do not resort to playing the victim or blame game. Get better by doing better; no excuses.

- Find a spiritually mature person you trust and discuss your feelings with him or her (venting friend). Talking with someone allows you to decompress those emotions.

MAINTAIN CONTROL

I love baseball; it's a great pastime. But, unfortunately, sometimes anger can get the best of a ballplayer. I've seen it many times.

When an angry player strikes out, he may have choice words

for the umpire. He may break the bat over his leg. He may even blame the pitcher and stare him down. When the batter gets to the dugout, he may throw his helmet or knock over the beverage cooler.

Sometimes the team manager gets angry over a bad call. He may come out of the dugout, approach the umpire, and begin to kick dirt at his leg while in his face yelling and spitting.

Ultimately, the display of anger by a ballplayer or team manager changes nothing. The call remains the same, and the ball game continues. What may have been altered, though, is the perception fans have of those individuals. Furthermore, in some instances, a team member gets thrown out of a game or fined, which may discourage him from openly expressing his anger in the future.

Anger doesn't grant you favor, but it does alter other's perception of you, which is often unfavorable. Unfortunately, an outburst of anger may never be forgotten. Benjamin Franklin said, "Whatever is begun in anger ends in shame." He also said, "Anger is never without a reason, but seldom a good one."

It's unfortunate that some people wander through life angry and offended because no one took time to teach or demonstrate love, self-control, patience, or to give wise counsel. If that describes your life currently, realize that anger and offense don't have to be carried into your future. You can change. You can choose to forgive and move on.

If your family is full of angry people and it's been that way for generations, you can put an end to the cycle of anger. Don't let

AVOID ANGER

another generation fall victim to the negativity that has lasted far too long. Choose to allow it to end with you.

From now on, choose to be a person who is slow to anger, as the Bible says in James 1:19. What does slow to anger mean to you? I'm sure it doesn't mean fast to anger, quick to anger, or soon to anger.

Slow to anger means being more longsuffering, having thick skin, staying extra cool, calm, and collected under pressure and in stressful conditions. It's not letting things get to you so easily. It's doing more smiling than frowning, more laughing than pouting, more controlled responses than uncontrolled reactions. It's being more forgiving than bitter. It's shutting your mouth instead of spouting off at the mouth. It means walking away instead of standing your ground. It means asking yourself if it's worth it.

To recap, we can't afford to let ourselves be so easily provoked. We can't allow people to get under our skin or control the thermostat of our lives. There will always be instigators, and they can't wait to take advantage of the opportunity to agitate us. We shouldn't empower them. Jesus is the only Lord in our lives, not anyone else.

Decide to settle issues before going to bed so you wake up fresh, over it, done with it, or else it will live another day. Apologize or resolve the matter. Make sure it's done from your heart and ask God to forgive you, if necessary.

Proverbs 19:11 (NLT) states, "Sensible people control their

239

temper; they earn respect by overlooking wrongs." Discretion and sensibility are huge when it comes to anger. Ask yourself, "Do I use discretion and sensibility? Is my anger restrained and thought out, or are my reactions uncontrolled and insensitive?"

The second part of Proverbs 19:11 mentions overlooking wrongs. To overlook an offense is a sign of emotional maturity. In other words, you see it, feel it, know it, hear it, but choose not to make a big deal about it. You show people grace; you give people the benefit of the doubt. You give others what they don't expect. You do for others what God did for you.

Prayer

Lord, I am sorry for the times I've allowed my anger to rise and take control of me. I realize that I have no excuse. The Spirit of God inside me is present to restrain me and produce the fruit of the Spirit in me. I now see that I have opened the door to the devil in the past by allowing wrong attitudes to be habitual in my life. Help me to walk in an awareness of the emotional collapse that can lead to lashing out or regretful reactions. Help me to overcome anger triggers. Your Word tells me not to let anger lead to sin. I will do this with the help of the Holy Spirit and the fruit of self-control.

I choose to shut the door to the devil so he can no longer find access to me, to my family, to my business, or any part of my life. To shut that door tight, I am asking You to help me overcome uncontrolled anger.

In Jesus' name. Amen.

Questions

If you have an anger issue, what would you say is the root cause?
Why do you get angry?

_____

_____

_____

_____

Who or what are your triggers; what sets you off?

_____

_____

_____

_____

Have you ever displayed righteous anger? If yes, explain.

_____

_____

_____

_____

Do you believe you can still act Christ-like when you become angry?

_____

_____

_____

_____

Additional Notes:

_____

_____

_____

_____

CHAPTER 8

OPPOSING OFFENSE

"It's a fact that it's much more comfortable to be in the position of the person who has been offended than to be the unfortunate cause of it."

—*Barbara Walters*

We're subjected to countless circumstances that can cause us to be offended—a report of injustice on the evening news, failed campaign promises from political figures, a reprimand from an employer, a honey-do task left undone by your spouse, a snide remark from the grocery store clerk, too many television commercials during your favorite program, junk mail, robocalls—the list is endless. We become offended by what was said, what was done, or what wasn't said or done to us. How someone looks or stares at us may offend us.

Even within the church world, Christians can become easily offended. Some take offense over changes in the worship service, including song selection and stage décor. Some take offense because ministries or departments cease to exist. There are those who become offended when the pastor doesn't acknowledge their contributions or achievements.

I remember someone taking offense because I made a joke that he didn't like. The person eventually left the church. In another instance, I spoke vividly about marriage and intimacy. Someone approached me and told me that she felt my approach to the subject matter was completely unnecessary. Another time, someone became offended because I used a fake name in my sermon, and he interpreted it as racist. Sometimes I refer to myself as a Mexican from Montebello, California, which I am. Even that offends people.

When we allow ourselves to fall prey to offense, we will fall short in being longsuffering (patient) toward the people who offended us and long in memory toward the perceived wrong. Notice that I used the words "perceived wrong." Sometimes, we misinterpret a situation. We assume something to be factual, but after closer examination, we find that it isn't.

When we feel offended, does all of the blame lie with others involved, or is it our suspicious nature, insecurities, or defensiveness that's at fault? That's a question we must consider, and it's one we'll examine a bit later in the chapter.

How many times have you thought something to be a fact but found out it wasn't? Well, it has happened to me.

I remember when I was dating my wife Cindy many years ago, and on one particular date, we went to a pizza restaurant. As we ate and talked, I noticed that she would look toward a guy in the restaurant's bar area every once in a while and blink her eyes at him. I thought, *You've got to be kidding me.* I was on a date with her, and I would pay for her meal. We were enjoying a great conversation, and she was attracted to someone else and was displaying it as we sat together.

The date came to an end, and I walked Cindy back to her car. As we approached her vehicle, something rose within me that I couldn't contain any longer. I had to ask her why she would do that. I was mad, offended, hurt, and disgusted, so I confronted Cindy about her actions.

To my accusation, Cindy replied, "I don't know what you're talking about."

I told her that I saw her blinking her eyes at the guy at the bar.

Cindy explained herself by saying, "I wear contact lenses. We were sitting under a fan, and the fan was drying out my lenses. I didn't want to look weird, so I turned away from you and looked toward the bar to try to adjust my focus by blinking my eyes. I didn't even notice a guy at the bar."

What I thought was one thing was actually something else. I was offended over a misperception. I was so grateful that Cindy went on another date with me after that one.

Maintaining a position of offense is a slippery slope, and it can be challenging to stop sliding once you start down that path. But, you can choose to forget the grudges you've held onto and give them over to the Lord. You can decide to tear down the barriers that separate you from people who've caused you pain and let the Lord heal you. You can choose to free yourself from the resentment you've carried and live a content and peaceful life.

UNDERSTANDING OFFENSE

It's challenging to maintain a relationship with someone who harbors offense because they don't let things go. They hold onto offenses like hoarders hold onto objects, like a dog covets a bone, like a monkey grips a banana. They talk about the offense as if it occurred yesterday, although it may have happened months or years ago.

Proverbs 18:19 states, "A brother offended is harder to win than a strong city, and contentions are like the bars of a castle." Figuratively, those who hold onto offenses have established a fortified city that's fully equipped with iron bars to hide behind and keep people at a distance. They are unable to let their guard down, which makes it hard for resolution to take place. They leave no room for forgiveness, grace, or love toward the offender.

Offended people make winning hard—winning opportunities, winning experiences, winning conversations, and winning relationships. Unfortunately, the opposite of a win is a loss, and when you allow offense to get to you, a loss of some sort is inevitable.

Offense affects people in different ways. Some people become confrontational when offended. Some isolate themselves, and some become overly suspicious and non-trusting of others. Some people become very cynical, especially in how they perceive particular groups of people, organizations, and situations.

Individuals like that are usually joyless, peaceless, and smileless, and, for them, letting go of past hurts, pains, unforgiveness, and bitterness is the road less traveled.

When offended, some people play the blame game or take on the role of victim. They are the ones who say, "I have a right." "It's not my fault." "I wouldn't be this way if it weren't for...." "Let him do what he is supposed to, and then I will." "Oh, woe is me." Generally speaking, when statements like that are made, the person making them is not seeking answers or an end to the offense. Instead, the person is staking his or her claim to remain in the state of offense. However, the blame game is not a game you want to play because there are no winners.

I believe pride plays a significant role when someone is offended. Pride says, "I am right; you're wrong." "What I think is more important than what you think." "I'm a better person than you."

What does the Bible say about pride? In Proverbs 16:18 (ERV), we read, "Pride is the first step toward destruction. Proud thoughts will lead you to defeat."

In the face of offense, what type of person are you?

A theologian named John Wesley said, "People who wish to be offended will always find some occasion for taking offense." In other words, one has to take (receive) offense to be offended. To take offense is an act of one's will. That means an individual can also choose to avoid, ignore, or let go of an offense.

Understanding that offense is a choice is a game changer, and choosing not to be offended is not as hard as some believe.

A well-known theologian named Martin Luther said, "You cannot keep birds from flying over your head, but you can keep them from building a nest in your hair." That's a creative way of saying some things are impossible, but not everything is unattainable.

When we can act responsibly, we should act responsibly. In other words, we can choose to be easily offended or quick to forgive. We can choose to have thin skin or thick skin. We can decide to make an issue out of everything or allow nothing to alter our Christian character unfavorably.

To take offense is like catching a baseball. You have to open your hands to catch it if that is your desire. You can choose not to catch offense when it's thrown your way. Don't sign for it, and don't respond to it. Don't answer the call when the phone rings if offense is on the other end of the line. Do just like a popular song says, "Return to sender." Don't interest yourself or become attracted to the offense.

CHANGE YOUR MIND

Knowing and applying the Word of God is the key to opposing and overcoming offense. Psalm 119:165 (KJV) says, "Great peace have they which love thy law: and nothing shall offend them."

The Word of God heals, changes, and delivers. It makes you peaceful and thankful. It ministers to you. When you're devoted to the light, love, and life found in the Word, how can you be easily offended?

When I think about it, I don't recall ever meeting a grateful, happy person who held onto offense very long. They just don't allow it to stick to them. In my opinion, they have too much to be thankful for, and they would prefer not to give any of their time to negative emotions, including offense.

I love the part of Psalm 119:165 that says, "Nothing shall offend them." Wow! Nothing?! Does that include a spouse, boss, co-worker, family member, and stranger? Yes, it does! It doesn't matter if it's big, small, unkind, hurtful, or belittling. It doesn't matter if it's morning, noon, or night. It doesn't matter if it's a weekday or the weekend. It doesn't matter if it's a holiday, vacation, birthday, or anniversary. Nothing shall offend those who love God's law.

I've committed Psalm 119:165 to memory. It has been a close, long-lasting friend to me and has helped me navigate many situations. It reminds me in difficult times not to be easily offended. I say to myself, "Diego, you're not easily offended. Nothing offends you because you love God's Word, which promises you peace." Wow! That's pretty liberating.

Learn daily to meditate on the Word of God. That means think about God's Word, study God's Word, believe God's Word, confess God's Word, and pray God's Word over your life. The reward of these disciplines is a renewed mind. That means your regular intake of God's Word will change your thought process.

Within time, as your mind is being renewed, you will begin to experience a transformation in your attitude. What once annoyed you will no longer do so as you gradually start to change. As healing takes place, you will find yourself becoming stronger, no longer vulnerable or susceptible to offense.

The Bible is filled with promises from God, promises that will encourage you and stretch your faith. I encourage you to seek them out in your daily devotion. The following are a few verses related to offense that you can confess over yourself.

> "Blessed is the man who remains steadfast under trial [offense], for when he has stood the test he will receive the crown of life, which God has promised to those who love Him."
>
> —James 1:12 (ESV)

> "Blessed are you when people hate you and when they exclude you and revile [offend] you and spurn your name as evil, on account of the Son of Man! Rejoice in that day, and leap for joy, for behold, your reward is great in heaven; for so their fathers did to the prophets."
>
> —Luke 6:22-23 (ESV)

> "For the sake of Christ, then, I am content with weaknesses, insults [offense], hardships, persecutions, and calamities. For when I am weak, then I am strong."
>
> —2 Corinthians 12:10 (ESV)

Barriers are built, walls of defense are erected, resistance is established when God's Word becomes your protective shield. Recall the famous words from the television series *Star Trek*, "Shields Up."

FROM RESENTMENT TO CONTENTMENT

I've carried offense several times since I became a Christian. One unforgettable and life-altering instance occurred while I was employed at my former church as an associate pastor.

I asked for and was granted a meeting with the senior pastor. I wanted to share how I was feeling about the call to ministry on my life. I respectfully informed the pastor that God was challenging me to leave that church (a place I had been for nine years) to start a church where I would be the senior pastor.

You may assume that was met with overwhelming support, encouragement, and lots of love, but that's not the case. Instead, as a result of sharing what was on my heart, my desk was cleared out within twenty-four hours. All my personal belongings were placed in a box that was handed to me, and I was told to go immediately.

That day I lost an annual income of $30,000. I lost friends. I wasn't allowed to say goodbye to anyone. I had no time to plan for that immediate disruption in my life. My thoughts were all over the place. I had no idea how I would provide for my wife, my small boys, and the household expenses.

I was genuinely offended. I felt like I had been kicked in the pants and told not to let the door hit me on the way out before it was slammed in my face. I felt betrayed, abandoned, put down, kicked out, and stomped on.

Initially, I had recurring thoughts about that incident, over and over, like Bill Murray in the movie *Groundhog Day*. The sting of it was like the bite of a rattlesnake.

I didn't want to hear the senior pastor's name mentioned. I didn't want to see or talk to the individual, and, to be honest, my heart was cold toward that person. I was offended with all the trimmings—hate, anger, bitterness, and unforgiveness.

As I think back, I realize that even though I had never been outwardly disrespectful or unethical toward the individual, I wasn't capable of letting go of that offense. I couldn't push past it, and that probably lasted six months.

I believe that, sometimes, God will allow you to feel the way you feel for a while, but then He will say, "That's enough! It's been long enough; get over it." It's the voice of the Father who wants you better and wants you healed. It's up to you whether you will obey or disobey Him.

I wish I had a better understanding of offense back then. It would have been better for me if I knew that it's okay to feel offended, but it's not okay for it to control me or extend its stay within my emotional makeup. I probably would have released it a lot sooner had I known more. I might not have carried it as long if I knew it was okay to express my feelings to a confidant. Instead, the offense I took on was seen in my actions. It became a part of my personality and lifestyle, and it was not acceptable.

Then it happened. I vividly remember, as if it were yesterday, hearing the gentle voice of the Holy Spirit telling me to "let it go." I was holding onto the offense like a vice, but I heard the

Holy Spirit say, "Enough!" Jesus wanted to heal me and deliver me from the hurt I was carrying.

God led me on a three-day prayer and fast to spend time with Him and reverse the self-imposed prison sentence. By the end of the three days, the prison bars were broken, I was broken, the offense was gone, and I was free. Thank God!

Like a scar, the memory is still there from my ordeal, but the sting, or the pain, associated with what took place is gone. I remember the brokenness I experienced, but I no longer carry the offense. I will forever be grateful for the mercy of God, for He knew that by holding onto that offense, I was hurting myself.

You may have physical scars that formed as a result of an injury. You remember experiencing the scrapes, stitches, or surgery, which left a mark, but the pain has long since ended. The same can be true of the offense you carry. Jesus wants to heal and deliver you from the pain you feel. The memory may remain, but not the sting. It may take effort, commitment, and faith, but that is a nominal cost for freedom.

THERE IS HOPE

Issues prevalent in our society today—political, global, economic, and social issues—can easily fuel the fire of offense, especially for those who live with shattered emotions. The gap between normalcy and their reality can appear too wide to shut for the offended person. Some people may require professional help because they see no end to the pain caused by offense.

There is no shame in seeking professional help. Although God is our source, He has made way for many resources to aid us in this life when it becomes necessary. I love what Proverbs 18:9 (AMPC) says: "He who is loose and slack in his work is brother to him who is a destroyer and he who does not use his endeavors to heal himself is brother to him who commits suicide."

As a pastor, I always tell people that their hope is in Jesus, and the simplicity of the Gospel of Jesus Christ is the best prescription I can offer anyone.

Romans 15:13 states, "Now may the God of hope fill you with all joy and peace in believing, that you may abound in hope by the power of the Holy Spirit." Who knows us better than God, our creator? When you have God's hope, you will possess peace and joy. Isn't that what every person wants?

Maybe you struggle with being offended, or you know someone who does. The Bible provides many stories about people who were offended for various reasons. I encourage you to take time to read the following accounts:

- Joseph's brothers were offended over a coat that Jacob, their father, gave to Joseph. (Genesis 37 NIV)

- Cain was offended over an offering that his brother Abel offered to God. He could have done the same. (Genesis 4:1-16 NIV)

- Sanballat, Tobiah, and Geshem were offended over Nehemiah rebuilding the walls of Jerusalem. They could have helped with the work. (Nehemiah 2:11-20 NIV)

- Aaron and Miriam were offended that Moses married an Ethiopian woman. It was none of their business. (Numbers 12:1-16 NIV)

- Jesus' disciples were offended that someone other than them was casting out demons in Jesus' name. Jesus wasn't offended. (Mark 9:38-39 NIV)

- Many followers of Jesus were offended at His hard teaching about His body and blood, which spoke of commitment and obedience. They departed from Him, never to return. (John 6:34-66 NIV)

My hope for the offended is that they seek and receive healing and deliverance. Unfortunately, unless they surrender to God and cry out to Him, many are destined to live a life of offense.

THE PATHWAY TOWARD DELIVERANCE

When you receive mail, do you look at the return address? Of course, you do. It's important to notice the sender of the letter. The return address provides a clue to the contents before the envelope is opened.

Understanding how, what, and why we are easily offended is a good starting point for healing to take place. Getting to the root cause of offense is the *aha* moment you must seek.

When I am delayed by another individual and forced to wait, I can become offended. When someone states that he or she doesn't like me, I can become offended. When someone doesn't respond quickly to a message I send, I can become offended. Initially, I didn't recognize these instances as triggers. Discovering my triggers required me to be intentional and seek honest answers about why I became offended.

What are your vulnerabilities? What are the triggers that cause you to become offended? What activates the desire to retreat from a Christ-like character? What drives you to abort the call to be light and salt in this world? These are questions I learned to ask myself during my experiences.

Your triggers may look like tiredness, hunger, disappointment, or unmet expectations. Is being compared to others something that triggers you? Is it how someone looks at you? Is it what someone says to you? Is it being cut off? Is it being ignored?

I encourage you to invite Jesus into your process of discovery. In John 8:12 (ESV), Jesus tells us, "I am the light of the world. Whoever follows me will not walk in darkness [or offense], but will have the light of life."

Acknowledge the Holy Spirit as your teacher, revealer, guide, counselor, and advocate. Allow the Holy Spirit to reveal why you get offended as well as why you separate yourself from people, and why you give up on commitments when you're offended. It's amazing how good He is at His job and how serious He takes His work.

Offense is all around us, and we have the potential to encounter it every day. It's like a rattlesnake that's hidden under a rock. If you don't stoop down to pick up the rock, you won't be bitten. Deciding not to take offense, or learning to forgive people quickly, can drastically reduce the likelihood of you becoming offended.

Predetermine that you will be a person who quickly forgives or considers what was said with an open mind. Settle within yourself that you will not be the type of person who quickly reacts negatively. Offense may come, but it doesn't have to stay.

I love the Bible because it contains situations that we can identify with today. There's a story found in scripture about two individuals involved in a confrontation. As I explain what occurred, I want you to place yourself in the story.

Imagine that someone very close to you, someone you admire, has been living a hypocritical life. He has been acting one way when around one group of friends but behaving differently when around a separate group. His hypocritical lifestyle and unhealthy influence are leading others astray.

Because he is your friend and you disagree with his actions, you decide to confront him. You feel he should know better because he seems to be a mature person. He has achieved amazing success and has an outstanding reputation as a leader in the church. He is considered to be a role model to many.

As I mentioned, this is a real situation found in the Bible. The actual individuals are Peter and Paul, and their story is found in Galatians 2:11-16.

Peter was the one living a hypocritical life, and Paul was the one who decided to confront him. Paul chose to confront Peter publicly instead of privately. He called him out in front of several others. When Peter was sternly reprimanded, he was likely embarrassed by Paul's open rebuke and ashamed of his hypocrisy.

After Paul's reprimand, Peter didn't become offended. What he endured may have hurt a lot, but Peter received Paul's correction. He repented after recognizing the error of his ways. He didn't become offended by Paul's words, his way of dealing with him publicly, Paul's facial expressions, or anything else that could have been considered offensive.

I love that Paul had the courage to stand up to his brother in the Lord and tell him the truth. I also love that Peter was humble and teachable and that he received the correction and changed. He did so without becoming hostile or taking offense. We can learn from Paul and Peter's ordeal and try to incorporate their approach in similar situations.

Our ultimate goal is to live an offense-free life amid disappointment. We will get upset sometimes, but the benefit of a renewed mind is that it won't go any further than that. An adverse circumstance will likely produce only a fleeting emotion that won't take root. A renewed mind won't allow negative emotions to become destructive.

FORGIVING THE OFFENDER

People can become so used to reacting in a particular way that they overlook what provokes adverse reactions. Most have probably had the same attitude and approach to life for years. Those who carry offense have likely endured great pain in the past. By neglecting the underlying issues, they experience deprivation of the soul (mind and emotions).

Offense is often clothed in pain, which can easily turn to anger, disapproval, and hatred toward others when ignited. Unfortunately, those negative emotions aren't only directed at the original offender but also at innocent, unsuspecting persons.

There was a time when I consistently felt let down by a particular person. I was expecting something from that individual like encouragement, compliments, support, an "I love you," a phone call, or text, but it wasn't happening. I did what I could to keep communication lines open, but my actions were not reciprocated; thus, I always felt offended. I searched within for answers to why, but I couldn't come up with any. One day, God revealed that I was looking for approval from someone who couldn't give me what they didn't have.

Offended people often direct what was done to them onto others. Until they are healed, they will continue to experience offense, but not necessarily as the offended but the offender. There's an old adage that speaks of that: "Hurting people hurt people."

What was done to them doesn't excuse their behavior, but being aware of their issue can prove helpful. For me, gaining an understanding of the situation was liberating.

After the revelation, I understood that only Jesus could fill the void within me. Only Jesus could heal me of disappointment and rejection. Colossians 2:10 (NIV) says, "So you also are complete through your union with Christ, who is the head over every ruler and authority." I knew from that point on that I was never to set myself up for disappointment over unmet expectations from anyone, and that understanding has served me well.

With my newfound perspective, God began to challenge me to be prepared for possible instances of offense. Being prepared and recognizing that people have various plights in life has helped me tremendously. John 2:24 (CEV) states, "But Jesus knew what was in their hearts, and he would not let them have power over him."

Additionally, I had to choose not to shop for offense. I know that the enemy will use someone or something to accommodate me if I do. Like food delivery services, they will deliver the offense on time, and it will be hot and ready for consumption.

God doesn't waste any of our life experiences. We may not understand them when we're going through them, but God always has a purpose. Romans 8:28 (NIV) says, "And we know that in all things God works for the good of those who love him, who have been called according to his purpose."

After years of counseling people, I know that everyone deserves a second chance. I know God gave me a second chance. Christianity is not about judging or kicking people to the curb. It's about God's redemptive love toward us, and we're to share that same love with others. 1 Corinthians 13:5 (NIV), speaking of love, states, "It does not dishonor others, it is not self-seeking, it is not easily angered, it keeps no record of wrongs."

If God's mercy and grace can heal our pain and restore us to wholeness and wellness, shouldn't we extend that same mercy and grace toward others? How can we drink water from God's well of forgiveness, mercy, and love that He has given to us so many times and not extend it to others?

To extend mercy, grace, love, and forgiveness toward others is a challenge for some. The reason being, they fail to see their own shortcomings—what God has forgiven of them—because they're focused on the failures of others. Like Jesus said in Matthew 7:5, "First remove the plank from your own eye, and then you will see clearly to remove the speck from your brother's eye."

Like I chose to do, decide to forgive everyone who disrespects, hurts, or betrays you. Do it today, and commit to it forever. It may be a long journey, but God is always faithful and always right on time. Today, I have love for my offender.

Keep in mind that forgiving someone is not the same as trusting someone. Trust is earned, but forgiveness is a gift that you can freely give away.

It's important to understand that fixing people is not our job. You can't change or help everyone, and you're not responsible for others' actions and decisions. That is especially so if a person is a perfectionist or is bent on controlling others and manipulating situations.

I wish everyone had ethics and morals, but not everyone does. Furthermore, not everyone has my style, discernment, values, or philosophy. I had to learn to let it go when people didn't do things the way I thought they should have been done.

Dr. Caroline Leaf, a communication pathologist and cognitive neuroscientist, said, "Not everyone thinks like you. What makes sense to you doesn't always make sense to someone else. What works for you may not work for someone else. That is why communication, patience, and empathy are vital."

LET IT GO

In many instances, an offender isn't aware that they've offended someone. Unfortunately, not all on the receiving end of an offense see it that way. When offended, consider giving people the benefit of the doubt. Maybe they didn't mean to offend. Not everyone is thinking about you all the time.

If someone meant to offend you, it's okay. People were always trying to offend Jesus. Some tried to distract Him from His mission by discouraging Him from doing ministry the way He was called to—God's way. Some wanted to hinder others from receiving God's message of provision, peace, joy, and love.

The following situations involved Jesus. In all of these circumstances, Jesus could have taken the bait of offense, but He didn't.

- Jesus could have been offended when Peter denied Him. (Matthew 26:69-75 NIV)

- Jesus could have been offended when Judas betrayed Him. (Matthew 26:15-16 NIV)

- Jesus could have been offended when the disciples deserted Him before His crucifixion. (Matthew 14:50 NIV)

- Jesus could have been offended when the people followed Him only for the fishes and loaves, healing and miracles. (John 6:26 NIV)

- Jesus could have been offended when the disciples couldn't heal the boy with a demon. (Mathew 17:14-20 NIV)

- Jesus could have been offended when his own family didn't believe in Him and thought He was crazy. (John 7:5 NIV)

- Jesus could have been offended at those on the streets of Jerusalem that cried, "Hosanna," but one week later were shouting, "Crucify Him." (Matthew 21:9, Luke 23:21 NIV)

- Jesus could have been offended when the disciples thought He didn't care about them on the Sea of Galilee. They asked, "Don't you care...?" (Mark 4:35-41 NIV)

- Jesus could have been offended at Thomas for doubting His resurrection. (John 20:24-29 NIV)

To walk in offense is to focus on situations that don't warrant our attention. Choosing to walk in offense also discourages us from being Christ-like. It's choosing to detach ourselves from Jesus, who is the source of love, joy, and peace in life. It's choosing to detach ourselves from God's assignments. It's choosing to cause a divide between us and the people we are meant to do life with.

Realize that the enemy knows you, and he will put people in your path that will push your offense buttons. The devil uses offense as a distraction; he has an objective in offense. The objective isn't to make Jesus our focus. It isn't to provoke us to make

Christ our example.

One definition for the word "offense" is a picture of a piece of wood propped up that, when moved, traps an animal in a cage. Offense can also be viewed as a rock or stone (1 Peter 2:8) that makes one trip or stumble, which never feels good.

Don't stumble over offenses. Don't be the person who gets caught up in the trap of offense and can't escape. Don't be caught off guard by people's attitudes or actions toward you. Don't be dumbfounded or flabbergasted by something someone did. What starts as disbelief that it happened progresses to disappointment, then to disgust, and finally offense. Misunderstanding will follow, and miscommunication is inevitable. Being prepared for what offense seeks to do to us, inwardly and outwardly, makes us wise.

No one is ever happy or healthy in their spirit and soul when they take hold of offense and choose not to let it go. When you let Jesus heal you of an offended spirit, you take away the enemy's power to keep you captive to offense. Division and strife will no longer govern your behavior. You will foil the enemy's plans to steal your God-given gifts and the fruit of your Christian faith—love, joy, peace, and patience—that is so desperately needed in our world today.

Accept that you are whole and sound in Jesus, not anyone or anything else. He completes you. He fills the empty, hollow places in your life.

Don't accept what God didn't intend for you. In the words from Disney's movie *Frozen*, "Let it go." Maintain your peace and joy by opposing offense.

Prayer

Father God, I repent for the offense I have harbored in my heart toward people. I see now that offense has held me in a prison of my own making. Your Word is very clear on how I am to respond to people who have hurt or offended me. I forgive my offenders, and I extend the same grace to them that I want others to give me. I will no longer be tormented by offense that has kept me from making spiritual progress as I should. I will no longer allow offense room to continue to festering in my heart and soul. Today, I choose to let it go.

When I am dealing with difficulties in relationships, You expect me to take the responsibility of hunting down peace and pursuing it. Help me always to keep the balanced perspective that I am to love the people. Help me find pathways into people's hearts, give them Your Word, and be a personal example that's so godly that they would want to imitate it. I ask You to show me what path I am to take in this pursuit so that I can please You. I receive Your help, Holy Spirit, to maintain a pure heart so that I not only can see God, but also so I see others as You see them.

In Jesus' name. Amen.

Questions

Have you ever perceived something as wrong but later discovered that your perception was false? How did you correct your actions?

_____

_____

_____

_____

What are the triggers that cause you to become offended?

_____

_____

_____

_____

How do you react when someone offends you? Do you believe your reaction is healthy or unhealthy?

_____

_____

_____

_____

John 2:24 (CEV) states, "But Jesus knew what was in their hearts, and he would not let them have power over him." What does this verse mean to you, and how can you apply it in your life?

_____

_____

_____

_____

Additional Notes:

_____

_____

_____

_____

Epilogue

If you or someone close to you is dealing with any of the destructive emotions discussed in this book, I want to encourage you. There is hope for you to live free from these emotions. That hope is found in Jesus Christ, and it starts by knowing Him and having a relationship with Him.

The Bible says in Romans 8:15, "For you did not receive the spirit of bondage again to fear, but you received the Spirit of adoption by whom we cry out, 'Abba, Father.'" Adoption is the message of the cross; it's taking those who are outside the family—without means, without care, less than—and bringing them into a relationship where someone takes responsibility for their life.

There are only two families in all creation; you either belong to the family of God or the family of the enemy called Satan.

Here's the reality: When Adam and Eve sinned against God, sin fell upon all humanity, which means our nature is sin. Though we can do good, our nature is sin. That's why God sent His son Jesus, who volunteered to be our sacrifice and our substitute, to redeem us and bring us back to the Father from our lost state.

The Bible states the following in John 3:16-17:

> For God so loved the world that He gave His only begotten Son, that whoever believes in Him should not perish but have everlasting life. For God did not send His Son into the world to condemn the world, but that the

world through Him might be saved.

God loves you, not because you're the best or the greatest; He just loves you.

In 1972, I was 11 years old, and I was a part of a little league team called the Mets. The Mets went 25 and 1 that year. We were the city champions, losing only one game. We lost that game because we had to forfeit, not because another team beat us. We didn't have enough guys to play that day.

Now, I'd like to brag about how influential I was on the team, and how the team wouldn't have won the championship without me. The truth, however, is I rode the bench. I was the kid they put in when the team was ahead. I was the kid they put in the outfield and hoped that nobody hit the ball to him. I was the kid who went up to the plate to bat, and the bat never left my shoulder. I was always a guaranteed out.

When the team portrait was taken and the championship trophy was presented, there I stood next to the MVP who batted better than anyone else in the league. I stood there next to the MVP pitcher who pitched no-hitters. I was part of the championship team, not because I earned it but because my uncle was the team's manager and coach.

When I signed up for little league, I was initially assigned to another team, but my uncle went to that team coach and said, "This is my nephew. I want him on my team." At that time, we didn't know that we would go 25 and 1 and win the championship, but we did!

That's what God did for you. You were on a losing team called damnation, hell, sin, and the devil. Your Heavenly Father reached out and chose you to be a part of His winning team, not because of your skill level or abilities. He just wanted to adopt you and have you on His team.

You were not purchased with silver or gold. You were bought with the shed blood of Jesus and adopted into the family. 2 Corinthians 5:21 says, "For He made Him who knew no sin to be sin for us, that we might become the righteousness of God in Him." That's how He purchased you. He became your sin—past, present, and future.

When you're adopted into the family of God, your nature and your future change. The Bible says in 2 Corinthians 5:17, "If any man be in Christ, he is a new creation; old things are passed away, and all things become new."

Adoption gives you full access to the Father's inheritance. Everything that the Father is and has become yours—His name, His reputation—all the benefits and privileges are bestowed on His children. That's what the Bible says is granted to you when you allow God to adopt you.

Some of the benefits you receive by being in the family of God are forgiveness, peace, joy, and grace—supernatural strength to make it through your toughest hour. That includes dealing with destructive emotions. He gives you the ability to use His name, and He has authority over the works of Satan.

One of the greatest benefits of being adopted into God's family is that your Father's home will one day become your home, which is called Heaven.

When God adopts you and becomes your Heavenly Father, it becomes final. Once you place your life in God's hands, no one will ever snatch you out of His hands.

God offers you forgiveness, peace, joy, grace, and eternal life. If you have not spoken to God about being a part of His family but want to be adopted, it can happen today. To begin your new life in Christ, state the following prayer:

Prayer of Salvation

Dear Lord Jesus, I'm a sinner who needs a Savior. I cannot save myself. So right now, I confess that Jesus Christ is the Lord and Savior of my life. I believe that He died on the cross for the forgiveness of my sins.

Thank you for adopting me into your family, Lord.

In Jesus' name. Amen.

Diego Mesa is the Founding Pastor of Patria Church in Rancho Cucamonga, CA, formerly known as Abundant Living Family Church. To learn more about Diego Mesa, including other books he has written, visit Diegomesa.org.

www.ingramcontent.com/pod-product-compliance
Lightning Source LLC
Chambersburg PA
CBHW070025100426
42740CB00013B/2594